NORTHAMPTON
TO
PETERBOROUGH

Vic Mitchell and Keith Smith

MP Middleton Press

Front cover: This is Wellingborough London Road in the 1960s. The driver is nearest to us as the push-pull unit is propelled towards us. Only the fireman remained on the engine in this direction on this economical system used widely for local trains. (LOSA)

Back cover: 1947 Railway Clearing House map.

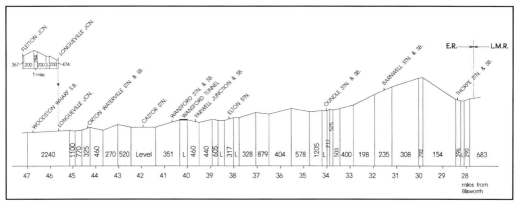

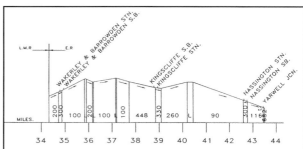

Published July 2016

ISBN 978 1 908174 92 5

© *Middleton Press, 2016*

Design   Deborah Esher
Typesetting Cassandra Morgan

Published by
        Middleton Press
        Easebourne Lane
        Midhurst
        West Sussex
        GU29 9AZ
Tel: 01730 813169
Email: info@middletonpress.co.uk
www.middletonpress.co.uk

Printed in the United Kingdom by Henry Ling Limited, at the Dorset Press, Dorchester, DT1 1HD

CONTENTS

INDEX

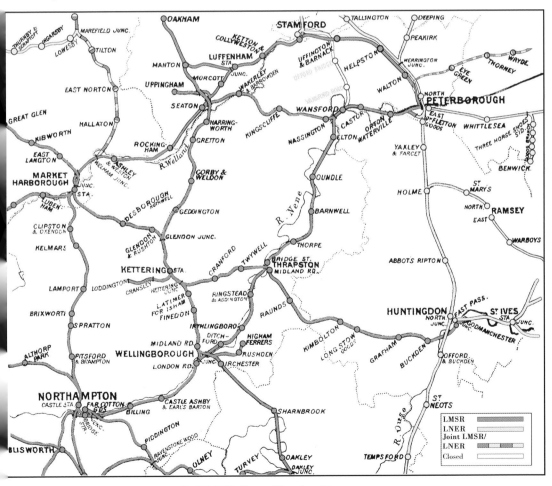

I. 1947 Railway Clearing House map.

GEOGRAPHICAL SETTING

Our main journey is in the valley of the River Nene, which is north flowing and within the county of Northamptonshire, to the locality of Wansford. Hereon, the river and the railway run east and over the borders of Rutland, Huntingdonshire and Cambridgeshire. The line crossed the Nene 13 times.

The route from Seaton to Wansford begins in the Welland Valley and climbs over the high ground carrying Rockingham Forest. The first part of it was in the southern area of Rutland.

The underlying geology of both routes is most complex, but includes clays suitable for brick production, in the Peterborough area. Ironstone was remunerative in the vicinity of Wakerley and Nassington in particular, for many years.

The maps are to the scale of 25ins to 1 mile, with north at the top, unless otherwise indicated.

NORTHAMPTON AND PETERBOROUGH RAILWAY.

Third Class between Northampton and Peterborough only.

Distance from Blisworth	TO PETERBOROUGH	DOWN TRAINS (except on Sundays)					Sundays.		Passengers' Fares. From Blisworth.		
		Morning.			Afternoon.		Morning.	Afternoon.	1st Class	2nd Cl	3 Class
		1, 2, & 3 Class.	1, 2, & 3 Class.	1, 2, & 3 Class.	1, 2, & 3 Class.	1, 2, & 3 Class.	1, 2, & 3 Class.	1 & 2 Class.			
Miles.		H. M.	H. M.	H. M.	H. M.	H. M.	H. M.	H. M.	s. d.	s. d.	s. d.
	TRAINS *leaving*										
	London at	—	7 30	10 45	4 0	8 30	7 30	8 30	—	—	—
	Birmingham at	—	7 0	10 30	4 0	—	—	—	—	—	—
4¾	Northampton { arrive	—	10 35	1 10	6 35	11 25	10 35	11 25	1 0	0 6	0 5
	{ leave	7 45	10 45	1 15	6 40	—	10 45	—			
11¾	Castle Ashby.......	7 55	10 55	—	6 50	—	10 55	—	2 0	1 6	1 0
15¾	Wellingborough....	8 15	11 15	1 45	7 10	11 55	11 15	11 55	2 6	2 0	1 4
17¾	Ditchford	8 18	11 18	—	7 13	—	11 18	—	3 0	2 6	1 6
20	Higham Ferrers ..	8 28	11 28	1 56	7 23	12 6	11 28	12 6	3 6	2 6	1 8
22¾	Ringstead	8 30	11 30	—	7 25	—	11 30	—	4 0	3 0	1 11
26	Thrapston	8 48	11 45	2 8	7 40	12 22	11 45	12 22	4 6	3 6	2 2
28¾	Thorpe	8 50	11 50	—	7 42	—	11 50	—	5 0	3 6	2 5
31¾	Barnwell	8 54	11 54	—	7 46	—	11 54	—	5 6	4 0	2 8
34¾	Oundle	9 8	12 8	2 17	8 0	12 40	12 8	12 40	6 0	4 6	2 11
40¾	Wansford (Silson)...	9 25	12 28	2 40	8 20	12 57	12 45	12 57	7 0	4 9	3 3
	Stamford (by Coach)	10 25	1 28	3 42	9 20	1 57	1 25	1 57	9 0	6 6	4 5
44¾	Overton	9 32	12 35	—	8 27	—	12 32	—	7 6	5 6	3 9
47¾	Peterborough	9 45	12 45	3 0	8 40	1 15	12 45	1 15	8 0	6 0	4 0

A Coach arrives at Wisbech from Peterborough, 6 30 p.m.

1845

ACKNOWLEDGEMENTS

We are very grateful for the assistance received from many of those mentioned in the credits, also from M.Back, J.Bonsall, A.J.Castledine, G.Croughton, G.Gartside, J.Horne, S.C.Jenkins, N.Langridge, B.Lewis, J.P.McCrickard, R.Owen, N.Sprinks, M.Turvey, T.Walsh, P.Waszak and in particular our always supportive families.

HISTORICAL BACKGROUND

The route was created as a branch of the 1838 London & Birmingham Railway and branched north from it near Blisworth. It was authorised under an Act of 1843 and opened to Northampton on 13th May 1845, reaching Peterborough on 2nd June of that year. The company became part of the London & North Western Railway in 1846.

At Northampton, a line was opened north to Market Harborough in 1859 by the LNWR. A connection south to Roade followed in 1881.

At Wellingborough, the Midland Railway opened from Hitchin and Bedford in the south and to Kettering and Market Harborough in the north, in 1857.

At Thrapstone, our route was crossed by the Kettering, Thrapstone & Huntingdon Railway in 1866. This became part of the MR in 1897.

At Yarwell Junction, a mile west of Wansford, the LNWR opened a route for passengers only to Seaton on 1st November 1879. Here it joined its 1851 line between Rockingham and Luffenham.

At Peterborough, the Eastern Counties Railway arrived from March on 14th January 1847. Other main lines opened thus: the MR from Stamford in 1846, the Great Northern Railway from Spalding in 1848 and its line from Huntingdon in 1850. Then came the GNR's route from Grantham in 1852 and finally the line from Eye and beyond in 1866.

The GER and GNR became part of the London & North Eastern Railway in 1923 and the MR and LNWR formed much of London Midland & Scottish Railway at the same time. The LNER became the main part of the Eastern Region of British Railways in 1948, while the LMSR formed most of the London Midland Region at this time of nationalisation.

Closure to passengers on the routes in this album took place thus: Northampton to Peterborough on 4th May 1964 and Seaton to Peterborough on 6th June 1966. The freight withdrawal details are given in the captions.

The reopening of the Wansford-Peterborough section by the Nene Valley Railway from 1977 onwards is detailed in the final section of this volume, from caption 103 to 118. The link south of Peterborough, from the west to the north, was open from 1881, but it did not have regular passenger services after 1914. It reopened in 1974 for stock transfer. Caption XVIII has more details.

PASSENGER SERVICES

The main route in this album provided the only direct link between London and Peterborough between 1845 and 1847. The first table below left reveals the details in 1847.

The frequency tables indicate the number of trains running on at least five days per week. The extracts show some of the others and many destinations.

Northampton to Peterborough				Seaton to Peterborough		
	Weekdays	Sundays			Weekdays	Sundays
1847	7	2		1881	5	0
1873	7	1		1902	9	1
1903	5	1		1925	7	1
1923	8	0		1945	7	1
1947	5	0		1965	7	0
1962	4	0				

Trains shown in the left table ran on the line to the east at Peterborough, the station being termed "East" from 1923.

Most trains in the right table were worked by the GNR, via the Fletton Curve northwards, into what was later to become Peterborough North. This route ceased to be used in 1914 and, thereafter, trains terminated at "East". They originated at Leicester Belgrave Road mostly and ran via Hallaton.

PETERBRO', MARKET HARBRO', and RUGBY.—L. & N. W.

Vauxhall Station,	mrn	mrn	mrn	b	Sat. only	aft
105 Yarmouth ..dep	....	6 0	8 10	1020		1 0
105 Norwich (Thorpe)	....	7 33	8 50	1115		2 5
Peterbro' ....dep	8 45	1030	1210	2 10	3 52	6 10
Wansford	8 57	1040	1220	2 22	4 4	6 22
Nassington..........	9 8	....	....	2 28	4 9	6 27
King's Cliffe ....[den	9 12	1050	....	2 37	4 16	6 35
Wakerley & Barrow-	9 22	....	....	2 47	4 24	6 44
Seaton 162..........	9 32	11 7	1247	2 57	4 33	6 56
Rockingham	9 41	....	a	3 7	4 41	7 4
Ashley and Weston..	9 51	....	a	3 18	4 50	7 14
Market Harbro' ar	10 2	1129	1 19	3 31	4 59	7 25
143, 162 dp	10 7	1131	1 21	3 35	5 1	7 26
Lubenham	1012	....	....	3 41	....	7 31
Theddingworth.. ..	....	....	....	3 48	....	a
Welford & Kilworth.	1024	1146	....	3 57	5 19	7 42
Yelvertoft & Stanford	....	1154	....	4 5	Sat. only	7 50
Lilbourne ... [Park	....	a	....	4 10		7 56
Clifton Mill [151, 231	....	....	....	4 18		....
Rugby 146, 164, arr	1037	12 5	1 50	4 25	5 37	8 5
147 Birmingham* arr	1215	1 20	3 30	5 45	6 55	9 25
147 Liverpool† .. ,,	2 15	3 10	5 0	7 45	8 50	3 0
198 Manchester‡ ,,	3 10	4 0	4 50	7 20	9 25	2 30

London Road Sta.,	mrn	b	mrn	aft	aft
198 Manchester dep	....	7 45	9 30	1 15	4 15
150 Liverpool† .. ,,	2 45	7 20	9 15	12 0	4 0
151 Birmingham* ,,	7 35	9 30	1140	4 0	6 0
Rugby ....dep	8 30	1050	1240	4 55	7 10
Clifton Mill	8 34	....	a	....	a
Lilbourne ....[Park	8 40	....	1249	....	7 20
Yelvertoft & Stanford	8 46	....	1254	....	7 26
Welford & Kilworth.	8 55	11 6	1 2	c	7 35
Theddingworth......	9 3	....	a	....	7 43
Lubenham	9 9	....	1 13	....	7 49
Market Harbro' ar	9 15	1121	1 19	5 22	7 55
Market Harbro' dp	9 17	1123	1 21	5 24	7 59
Ashley and Weston..	9 28	1132	1 31	a	8 9
Rockingham	9 40	1142	1 42	a	8 20
Seaton ....[den	9 51	1152	1 54	5 54	8 31
Wakerley & Barrow-	9 59	....	2 4	a	8 39
King's Cliffe	10 9	12 8	2 14	6 10	8 49
Nassington..........	1018	....	2 23	....	8 58
Wansford 161, 135	1024	1220	2 29	6 22	9 4
Petrbro' 106, 107, 133	1040	1233	2 45	6 35	9 20
Norwich 104 arr	....	3 2	6 20	....	2 0
104 Yarmouth ,,	....	3 35	7 0	....	3 0

* New Street. † Lime Street. ‡ London Road.

a Stop by signal to take up, and set down on informing the Guard at the preceding *stopping* Station. **b** Through carriages between Yarmouth and Birmingham. **c** Stops when required to set down from London.

August 1881

RUGBY, MARKET HARBRO', UPPINGHAM, STAMFORD, & PETERBRO'.—London & North Western

Miles frm Rugby.	Euston Station,	ngt.	mrn	mrn	mrn	aft	aft	aft	aft	aft	SUNDAYS. ngt.	SUNDAYS. aft
	London 360 ..dep.	12 0	5 15	8 35	1015	....	2 45	....	4 5	6 30	12 0	5 30
	442 Liverpool* .. " h	1045	2 35	7 15	9 45	....	2 0	....	....	5 25	1045	4 5
	456 Manchester†. "	1050	1155	8 30	10 0	....	2 10	....	....	5 32	1050	4 25
	381 Birmingham‡. "	1250	7 30	10 0	1150	....	4 0	....	....	7 0	1250 (Sats.)	5 50
—	Rugby ....dep.	2 40	8 30	1110	1 0	Fridays only.	5 10	....	6 0	8 35	2 40	7 30
1	Clifton Mill	mrn	8 34	....	1 5		....	....	6 5	8 40	mrn	7 35
3¼	Lilbourne ....[Park	....	8 40	....	1 12		....	....	6 11	8 46	....	7 41
5¼	Yelvertoft & Stanford	....	8 45	....	1 18		....	....	6 16	8 51	....	7 46
9¼	Welford & Lutterworth	....	8 54	1124	1 26		5 23	....	6 24	8 59	....	7 55
12½	Theddingworth	....	9 2	....	1 36		....	....	6 33	9 8	....	8 3
14¼	Lubenham ..[319, 480	....	9 6	....	1 41		....	....	6 38	9 14	....	8 8
17¾	Market Harbro' arr.	3 5	9 12	1136	1 47		5 38	....	6 45	9 22	3 5	8 15
—	360 London (Eus.).dep.	12 0	5 15	9 20	1015		2 45	2 45	....	7 0	12 0	....
—	Market Harbro' ..dep.	3 7	9 16	1144	1 53		5 39	5 44	....	9 32	3 7	....
22¼	Ashley and Weston....	....	9 27	1152	2 3			5 55	....	9 42	....	....
27¼	Rockingham	....	9 38	12 1	2 13			6 6	....	9 52	....	....
31½	Seaton 325 ....arr.	3 30	9 47	12 8	2 21			6 16	....	9 59	3 30	....
—	Seaton ....dep.	....	9 54	1215	2 35	5 20	Harwich Express.	6 17	....	....	....	....
35	Uppingham ..arr.	....	10 5	1225	2 45	5 30		6 27	....	....	....	....
—	Seaton ....dep.	3 33	9 50	1210	2 30	....		6 19	....	10 2	3 33	....
33½	Morcott	....	9 55	1215	2 35	....		6 24	....	10 7	....	....
36¼	Luffenham 516......	....	10 0	1219	2 40	....		6 28	....	1011	....	....
37¾	Ketton	....	10 7	1225	2 45	....		6 34	....	1017	....	....
41½	Stamford 328, 308.	3 50	1016	1233	2 53	....		6 42	....	1025	3 50	....
34¼	Wakerley & Barrowden	....	9 56	....	2 30	....	....	....	....	10 7	....	....
38¼	King's Cliffe	....	10 5	1220	2 38	....	6 11	....	....	1015	....	....
42¼	Nassington	....	1014	....	2 46	....	....	....	....	1023	....	....
44¼	Wansford 328, 376...	3 53	1019	1228	2 48	....	d	....	....	1026	3 53	....
45¼	Castor..................	....	1024	....	....	....	....	....	....	....	....	....
47¾	Overton ....[308, 294	....	....	....	2 57	....	....	....	....	....	....	....
50¼	Peterbro' 246, 244, ar	4 5	1037	1240	3 5	....	6 30	....	....	1040	4 5	....
134¼	Norwich 240. arr.	1035	....	3 50	6 29	....	10 0	....	....	2 0	....	....
154¼	Yarmouth 240 "	12 8	....	4 52	7 15	....	1051	....	....	3 0	....	....

a Stops by signal to take up for Market Harbro' and beyond. **b** Stops to set down from Peterbro' and beyond on informing the Guard at Market Harbro'. **c** Arrives at 2 58 mrn. on Sundays. **d** Stops to set down from Rugby and beyond on informing the Guard at Market Harbro'. **e** 1st & 3rd class. **g** Arrives at 3 10 mrn. on Sundays.

December 1902

PETERBRO', SEATON, and LEICESTER.—Great Northern.

Mls	Down.	mrn	aft	aft
—	Peterbro' (G.N.) dep.	9 31	2 15	7 24
3¼	Overton	9 38	2 22	7 31
5½	Castor	9 43	2 27	7 36
7	Wansford 328	9 48	2 32	7 41
8¾	Nassington..........	9 52	2 36	7 45
12¾	King's Cliffe	10 0	2 44	7 53
17	Wakerley & Barrowdn	10 8	2 52	8 1
20	Seaton	1014	2 58	8 7
24	Rockingham	1022	3 6	8 15
28¾	Medbourne..........	1031	3 15	8 24
30¾	Hallaton	1036	3 20	8 29
33	East Norton	1041	3 25	8 34
37	Tilton 319..........	1049	3 33	8 42
39¾	Loseby	1055	3 39	a
42¼	Ingersby, fr Houghtn	11 1	3 44	a
45¼	Thurnby & Scraptoft.	11 7	3 50	a
47¾	Humberstone	1113	3 56	9 0
49	Leicester (Belgrve R.)	1118	4 1	9 5

Mls	Belgrave Road,	mrn	mrn	aft
—	Leicester ......dep.	7 5	1020	4 0
1¼	Humberstone	7 9	1024	4 4
3¼	Thurnby & Scraptoft.	7 14	1029	4 10
6½	Ingersby, fr Houghtn	7 21	1036	4 16
9¼	Loseby	7 27	1042	4 22
12	Tilton	7 33	1048	4 28
16	East Norton	7 40	1055	4 35
18¼	Hallaton	7 45	11 0	4 40
20¼	Medbourne..........	7 50	11 5	4 45
25	Rockingham	7 58	1113	4 53
29	Seaton 379..........	8 6	1121	5 5
32	Wakerley & Barrowdn	8 12	1127	5 11
36½	King's Cliffe	8 19	1135	5 19
40¼	Nassington..........	8 26	1143	5 27
42	Wansford 328	8 30	1147	5 31
43½	Castor ... [244, 246	8 34	1151	....
45¾	Overton ..[313, 294,	8 40	1157	....
49	Peterbro' (G.N.) arr.	8 49	12 6	5 45

a Stops to set down on informing the Guard at the preceding *stopping* Station.

December 1902

RUGBY, MARKET HARBORO', UPPINGHAM, STAMFORD, and PETERBRO'.—L. M. & S.

Miles from Rugby.	Down.	Week Days.																	Sundays.			
		ngt.	mrn	mrn	mrn	mrn	mrn	aft	mrn	mrn	aft		aft	aft	aft	aft	aft	aft	ngt.	aft		
	304London (Euston)..dep.	11 50	....	2 35	....	5 0	....	....	10 0	1035	....		2 50	....	....	4 0	....	7 0	12F10	6 0	....	....
	316Liverpool (L.S.).. "	....	....	2a25	....	....	....	....	8 5	9 40	....		2 0	....	....	2 45	....	4 0	....	3 55	....	....
	316Manchester (L.R.) "	....	....	12d0	....	....	....	....	8 15	1010	....		1h15	....	2 30	2 50	....	4n30	....	4 20	....	....
	369Birmingham (N.S.) "	12 15	....	1215	R	7 30	....	....	1013	1140	....		4 4	....	....	4 58	....	7 5	12F15	5 15	....	....
	Rugby..............dep.	2 40	....	6 35	....	8 30	....	....	1217	1 0	....		4 56	....	5 15	6 23	....	8 50	2 40	7 45	....	....
1	Clifton Mill A..........	mrn	....	6 38	....	8 34	....	....	1224	1 4	....		....	....	5 19	6 31	....	8 59	Sun	7 49	....	....
3½	Lilbourne..............	Except Mondays	....	6 44	7 48	8 40	....	....	1231	1 9	....		Gg	....	5 25	6 37	....	9 5	mrn	7 55	....	....
5½	Yelvertoft & Stanford Park		....	6 49	7 55	8 45	....	....	1236	1 15	....		....	....	5 30	6 42	....	9 10	....	7 59	....	....
9½	Welford and Kilworth B..		....	6 57	8 15	8 53	....	....	1245	1 26	....		Hh	....	5 39	6 52	....	9 17	....	8 10	....	....
12½	Theddingworth..........		....	7 4	8 25	9 0	....	....	1252	1 37	....		5s18	....	5 48	7 3	....	9 26	....	8 21	....	....
14½	Lubenham.....[536, 717		....	7 9	8 32	9 5	....	....	1258	1 44	....		....	....	5 53	7 8	....	9 31	....	8 26	....	....
17½	Market Harboro' 363, arr.	3 5	....	7 16	8 40	9 11	....	....	1 5	1 50	....		5 32	....	6 0	7 15	....	9 37	3 5	8 32	....	....
—	363London (Euston)..dep.	....	....	5 0	....	....	....	....	Saturdays only.	9 30	....	Through Carriage, Birmingham to Harwich, see pages 369, 759, 756, and 749.	3 5	....		....	....	7 0	....	....	....	....
—	Market Harboro'....dep.	3 10	....	7 28	....	9 20	1018	....		2 2	....		5 35	5 50	Except Saturdays.	....	....	9 41	3 10	....	....	....
22½	Ashley and Weston C.....	....	....	7 37	....	9 30	1026	....		2 12	....		....	5 59		....	....	9 50	....	....	....	....
27½	Rockingham..............	....	....	7 47	....	9 40	1036	....		2 22	....		....	6 9		....	....	9 59	....	....	....	....
31½	Seaton D............arr.	3 29	....	7 55	....	9 49	1044	....		2 31	....		....	6 16		....	....	10 7	3 29	....	....	....
—	Seaton............dep.	....	....	8 10	....	....	1047	1225		2 48	5 5		....	6 22		....	7 12	....	....	....	....	....
35	Uppingham.......arr.	....	....	8 23	....	....	1057	1235		2 58	5 15		....	6 32		....	7 22	....	....	....	....	....
—	Seaton............dep.	....	6 35	8 15	....	10 5	....	1220	....	2 50	....		....	6 30	....	....	....	....	....	....	....	....
33½	Morcott..............	....	6 40	8 20	....	1010	....	1225	....	2 56	....		....	6 36	....	....	....	....	....	....	....	....
35½	Luffenham 591..........	....	6 52	8 24	....	1014	....	1230	....	3 1	....		....	6 41	....	....	....	....	....	....	....	....
37½	Ketton............[733	....	6 58	8 30	....	1020	....	1236	....	3 7	....		....	6 47	....	....	....	....	....	....	....	....
41½	Stamford 590, 691, arr.	....	7 5	8 36	....	1027	....	1241	....	3 15	....		....	6 55	....	....	....	....	....	....	....	....
—	Seaton..............dep.	3 31	....	7 56	....	9 51				2 33	....		5X53	6 17	....	....	....	10 8	3 31	....	....	....
34½	Wakerley and Barrowden..	....	....	8 1	....	9 58				2 40	....		....	6 24	....	....	....	1015	....	....	....	....
38½	King's Cliffe..........	....	....	8 9	....	10 7				2 49	....		6X2	6 33	....	....	....	1023	....	....	....	....
42½	Nassington..............	....	....	8 17	....	1016				2 58	....		....	6 41	....	....	....	1031	....	....	....	....
44½	Wansford 363, 733......	3 53	....	8 22	....	1021				3 3	....		6X12	6 46	....	....	....	1036	3 53	....	....	....
45½	Castor............[759	....	....	....	....	1026				....	....		....	6 51	....	....	....	....	....	....	....	....
47½	Orton Waterville...[695,	....	....	....	....	1031				3 11	....		....	6 56	....	....	....	....	....	....	....	....
50½	Peterbro' J....688, arr.	4 5	....	8 35	....	1040				3 20	....		6 25	7 5	....	....	....	1050	4 5	....	....	....
184	759Norwich (Thorpe). arr.	10 38	....	1222	....	3 27	....	....	....	5 41	....		9 38	....	....	....	....	1 58	7 38	aft.	....	....
151½	759Yarmouth (Vaux.) "	12 22	....	1 14	....	4 37	....	....	....	6 46	....		1034	....	....	....	....	3 0	8 39		....	....
134½	759Ipswich 756...... "	10 33	....	1 8	....	4 31	....	....	....	6 5	....		9 3	....	....	....	....	....	7 47		....	....
153	749Harwich (P.Q.)... "	11l26	....	2b14	....	5 48	....	....	....	9B0	....		9 38	....	....	....	....	....	9 5		....	....
155	759 " (Town).. "	11l35	....	2b25	....	5 57	....	....	....	9B10	....		9 51	....	....	....	....	....	9 20		....	....

A Clifton-on-Dunsmore.
a Departs Liverpool at 10 50 aft. on Sundays.
B Station for Husbands Bosworth; Station near North Kilworth, 2¼ miles from Welford.
B Arrives Harwich (Parkeston Quay) at 7 59 and Harwich (Town) at 8 8 aft. on Saturdays.
b Arrives Harwich (Parkeston Quay) 2 4 aft., Harwich (Town) at 2 15 aft. on Saturdays.
C Station for Medbourne (1 mile).
D ¾ mile to Harringworth.
d Departs Manchester at 11 40 aft. on Sundays.
F Saturday nights.
Gg Calls at Lilbourne when required to take up for beyond Market Harboro' on notice being given at the Station.
Hh Stops on Saturdays at 5 11 aft.; on other days when required to take up for beyond Market Harboro' on notice being given at the Station.
h Departs Manchester (London Road) at 1 32 aft. on Saturdays.
J Peterbro' (East, L. & N. E.).
l Via Bishop's Stortford, Dunmow, and Witham.
n Departs Manchester (London Road) at 4 10 aft. on Saturdays.
R Mondays only.
X Stops to take up for beyond Peterbro' on notice being given at the Stations.

September 1925

RUGBY, MARKET HARBORO', UPPINGHAM, STAMFORD, and PETERBRO'

Miles from Rugby	Down	Week Days																				Sn.
		ngt.	ngt.	mrn	mn	mrn	aft	mrn	aft	mrn	aft	aft	aft	aft		aft	aft	aft	aft	aft	aft	aft	mrn
	412London (Euston)..dep.	1155	11 55	..	..	..	..	10 25	..	10 45	..	..	..	1 5		2 50	3 6	..	..	4 0	4 55	5 10	11F55
	424Liverpool (L.St.).. "	12 2	12 30	..	..	..	..	8 5	..	10 0	..	..	..	1145		2 0	..	..	..	..	2 50	5 25	12F2
	424Manchester (L.Rd.) "	12 5	12 5	..	..	..	..	7 55	..	10 20	..	..	..	1155		2 15	..	..	..	..	3‡20	5 35	12F5
	475Birmingham (N.St.) "	..	..	3 55	..	..	..	10 23	..	10Z52	..	..	..	3H25		..	..	..	..	5 0	5 23	7 47	12 20
		mrn	mrn	mrn	mn	mrn	aft	aft	aft	aft	aft	aft	aft	aft		aft	aft	aft	aft	aft	aft	aft	mrn
	Rugby..............dep.	4 0	6 29	7 23	..	..	..	12 20	..	1 35	..	..	..	4 25		4 50	5 28	..	..	6 50	7 20	9 5	4 0
1	Clifton Mill A..........	Except Mondays	..	7 25	..	..	..	12 22	..	1 37	..	..	..	..	Through Carriage Rugby to Yarmouth and Lowestoft (arr 11 49 aft.)	..	5 35	From Northampton	..	6 52	7 22	..	..
3½	Lilbourne..............		..	7 31	..	..	..	12 28	..	1 43	..	..	..	..		..	5 41		..	6 58	7 28	..	..
5½	Yelvertoft & Stanford Park		6 38	7 36	..	..	..	12 33	..	1 48	..	..	..	..		..	5 46		..	7 3	7 33	..	..
9½	Welford and Kilworth B..		6 47	7 45	..	..	..	12 43	..	1 57	..	..	..	4 40		..	5 56		..	7 12	7 43	9 24	..
12½	Theddingworth..........		6 53	7 51	..	..	..	12 49	..	2 3	..	..	..	..		..	6 3		..	7 18	7 49	..	..
14½	Lubenham ..[642, 897b		6 58	7 56	..	..	..	12 54	..	2 8	..	..	..	..		..	6 8		..	7 23	7 54	9 33	..
17½	Market Harboro' (below) ar	4 25	7 5	8 3	..	..	..	1 1	..	2 16	..	..	..	4 53		5 17	6 15		..	7 30	8 1	9 41	4 25
—	642London (St. Pan.).dep.	..	4 20	Stop	..	..	..	10 0	..	12 0	..	..	..	..		3 0	..	4 5	..	..	Except Sats.	6 35	..
—	" (Euston).. "	..	..		..	..	..	..	..	11 35	..	..	..	..		..	..	3 6	..	..		5 10	..
—	Northampton (Cstle) "	1V36	6 40	..	..	..	..	10V36	..	1 20	..	..	..	2V55		..	..	5 29	..	Saturdays only		8 28	1V28
—	649Leicester (L.Rd.) "	2 38	5 55	..	..	..	..	11 26	..	1 0	..	..	..	2 35		4 50	..	..	..			9 8	2 36
—	Market Harboro'....dep.	4 45	7 33	..	..	..	..	1 7	..	2 23	..	..	..	4 58		5 27	..	6 21	..			9 51	4 45
22½	Ashley and Weston C.....	..	7 40	..	..	..	..	1 14	..	2 30	..	..	..	..		..	..	6 28	..			9R58	..
27½	Rockingham..............	..	7 48	..	..	..	..	1 22	..	2 38	..	..	..	..		5 41	..	6 36	..		Stop	10J6	..
31½	Seaton D............arr.	..	7 56	..	..	..	..	1 30	..	2 46	..	..	..	5 17		5 49	..	6 44	..		aft	1014	5 5
—	Seaton............dep.	..	8 3	..	9 40	11 31	..		2 15	2 55	..	..	4 53	..		..	..	6 49	..		8 40	..	..
35	Uppingham.......arr.	..	8 12	mrn	9 50	11 41	..		2 24	3 5	..	..	5 1	..		..	..	6 58	..		8 49	..	..
—	Seaton............dep.	..	..	8 25	..	..	1240	Sats. only	..	..	310	4 0	..	5 30		..	..	..	713	..	..	..	..
33½	Morcott..............	..	..	8 29	..	..	1244		..	..	314	4 4	..	5 34		..	..	..	..	..	..	..	..
35½	Luffenham 690..........	..	..	8 33	..	..	1248		..	..	318	4 9	..	5 38		..	..	..	720	..	..	..	..
37½	Ketton and Collyweston.	..	..	8 38	..	..	1253		..	..	323	..	..	5 43		..	..	..	..	..	..	..	..
41½	Stamford 690, 886. arr.	..	..	8 45	..	..	1 0		..	..	330	..	..	5 50		..	..	..	730	..	..	..	..
—	Seaton..............dep.	..	7 59	..	..	..	..	1 35	..	2 50	..	..	..	5 20		5 51	..	6 47	..	..	..	1017	5 8
34½	Wakerley and Barrowden..	..	8 3	..	..	..	..	1 39	..	2 54	..	..	..	..		..	..	6 51	..	..	..	..	..
38½	King's Cliffe..........	..	8 12	..	..	..	..	1 48	..	3 3	..	..	..	..		6 3	..	7 0	..	..	..	1028	..
42½	Nassington..............	..	8 19	..	..	..	..	1 55	..	3 10	..	..	..	..		..	..	7 7	..	..	..	..	..
44½	Wansford 472...........	..	8 24	..	..	..	..	..	..	3 14	..	..	..	5 37		6 15	..	7 11	..	..	..	1039	..
45½	Castor............[873	..	..	..	..	..	..	..	..	3 18	..	..	..	..		..	..	..	..	..	..	..	..
47½	Orton Waterville...[821,	..	..	..	..	..	..	..	..	..	..	..	..	..		..	..	..	..	..	..	..	..
50½	Peterbro' J 810, arr.	5 35	8 39	..	..	..	..	2 15	..	3 35	..	..	..	5 55		6 30	..	7 22	..	..	..	1050	5 38
134	873Norwich (Th.) ..arr.	1048	12 0	..	..	..	..	5 31	..	..	..	..	..	..		10 20	..	2U36	..	..	..	3P30	12 K0
151½	879Yarmouth (V.) .. "	1148	1 39	..	..	..	..	6 25	..	..	..	..	..	..		11 42	..	4S36	..	..	..	..	1†39
134½	869Ipswich .... "	1020	1 23	..	..	..	..	5 45	..	..	..	..	..	..		9 59	..	1S58	..	..	..	..	9 42
153	864Harwich (P.Q.) .. "	1223	3L28	..	..	..	..	6 43	..	..	..	..	..	..		10*54	..	..	..	..	..	..	11 13
155	873 " (Town) "	1233	3L38	..	..	..	..	6 53	..	..	..	..	..	..		11* 5	..	..	..	..	..	..	11 23

A Clifton-on-Dunsmore
B Station for Husbands Bosworth station near North Kilworth, 2¼ miles from Welford
B Except Sunday' morns.
C Station for Medbourne (1 mile)
D ¾ mile to Harringworth
E Except Saturdays,
F Saturday nights
H Thro' Carriages Birmingham to Peterboro' (East).
J Peterborough (East, L.N.E.)
J Calls except Sats. to set down only on notice being given at Market Harborough. On Sats. only calls unconditionally
K Noon.
L Via Sudbury
P Sunday morns. only
R Calls regularly on Sats. and on Tues., & Fris. to set down only on notice being given at Market Harborough
S Saturdays only
U Except Sunday morns. Via Haughley
V Via Rugby
Z Dep. 12 30 aft on Sats.
* 4 mins. later on Sats. † Aft
‡ Mayfield Station

January 1945

1. Northampton to Peterborough

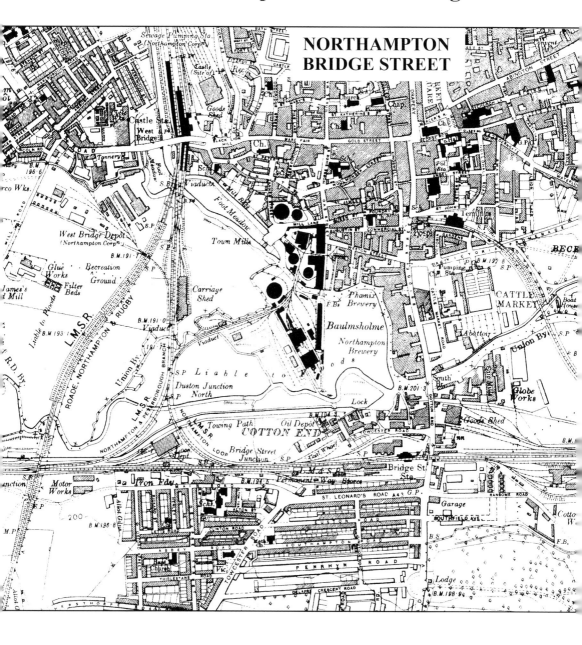

NORTHAMPTON BRIDGE STREET

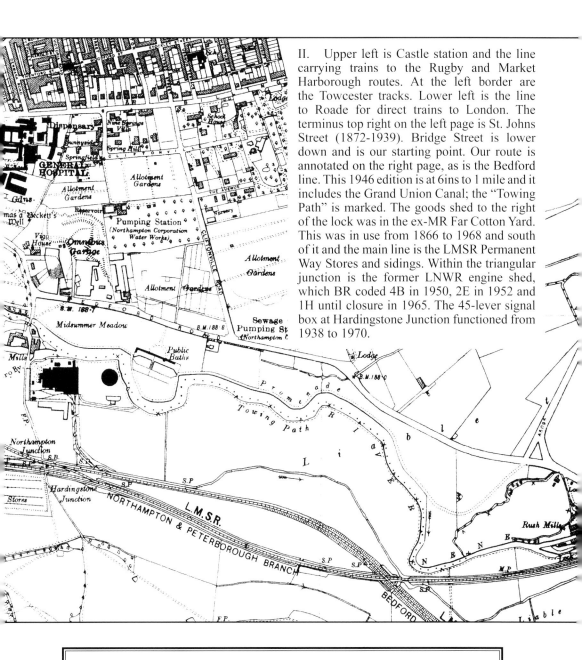

II. Upper left is Castle station and the line carrying trains to the Rugby and Market Harborough routes. At the left border are the Towcester tracks. Lower left is the line to Roade for direct trains to London. The terminus top right on the left page is St. Johns Street (1872-1939). Bridge Street is lower down and is our starting point. Our route is annotated on the right page, as is the Bedford line. This 1946 edition is at 6ins to 1 mile and it includes the Grand Union Canal; the "Towing Path" is marked. The goods shed to the right of the lock was in the ex-MR Far Cotton Yard. This was in use from 1866 to 1968 and south of it and the main line is the LMSR Permanent Way Stores and sidings. Within the triangular junction is the former LNWR engine shed, which BR coded 4B in 1950, 2E in 1952 and 1H until closure in 1965. The 45-lever signal box at Hardingstone Junction functioned from 1938 to 1970.

Castle station is illustrated in *Bletchley to Rugby* **(nos 61 to 70) and** *Wellingborough to Leicester* **(nos 96 to 100). St John's Street is in** *Bedford to Wellingborough* **(nos 65 to 67).**

1.   A view east from the footbridge has one level crossing post, plus part of the original station building. A train from Peterborough is arriving in 1943, hauled by class F1 4-4-0 no. 1028 on loan from the Southern Railway. (A.W.V.Mace/R.S.Carpenter)

2.   We look west from the level crossing and the Bridge Street Junction signals are in the distance. The goods yard is crowded on the right, while cattle wagons rest on the left. The suffix was added in June 1876. (LOSA)

3. Class 2P 4-4-0 no. 353 arrives from the east, prior to receiving a BR number in March 1949. The class originated in 1882. Above the cab is the dairy chimney. (SLS coll.)

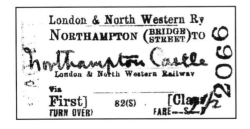

London & North Western Ry
NORTHAMPTON (BRIDGE STREET) TO

Northampton Castle

London & North Western Railway

Via

First]   82(S)   [Class
TURN OVER)   FARE

2066

3rd · SINGLE   SINGLE · 3rd

NORTHAMPTON
(BRIDGE STREET) TO

Northampton   Northampton
(Bridge Street)   (Bridge Street)
Northampton   Northampton
(Castle)   (Castle)

NORTHAMPTON (CASTLE)

(M) 0/2 H   Fare   0/2 H (M)

For conditions see over   For conditions see over

1604   1604

4.   The scroll brackets for the platform canopies are not clear in most photographs, but we can enjoy them here on 29th June 1955. In the background is the cooling tower of the power station. This was served by a siding from Northampton Junction, shown near the left border of the right map. (H.C.Casserley)

5.   The stone balustrades between the two ornate gables are fine features, which are difficult to see from the platforms. More of the main goods yard is evident beyond the platforms on 4th March 1961. Beyond the left signals is the coaling plant at the locomotive depot. (Millbrook House)

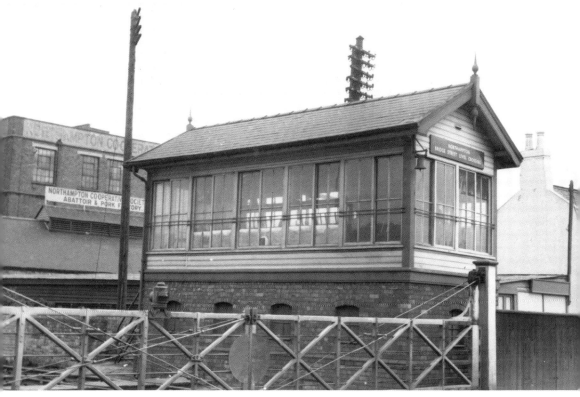

6. Seen in April 1965 is the crossing, which was the cause of much road traffic delay, as many passenger trains stood on it. The box opened in 1907 and replaced two earlier boxes. Its frame had 35 levers. (R.J.Essery/R.S.Carpenter)

7. The station closed to passengers on 4th May 1964. The line through Bridge Street remained open after that for various departmental traffic flows, serving Bridge Street Pre-Fab Depot (Civil Engineer), Central Materials Depot (Civil Engineer) and Geismar UK Ltd. No. 25205 passes Bridge Street level crossing westbound with a special train of track sections from Northampton Central Materials Depot on 16th April 1986. (P.D.Shannon)

8.   The extension to Brackmills closed officially in September 1988. The remaining traffic to and from Bridge Street gradually declined until formal closure of the branch from Northampton Castle in 2005. Bridge Street box was burnt out on 15th April 2006 and then demolished. No. 31121 departs from Bridge Street with an engineers train from Northampton Central Materials Depot on 14th August 1987. The inclusion of a ferry van in this train was unusual. The shed had been used for engines until 1881, when they were all based at Castle. (P.D.Shannon)

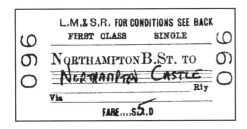

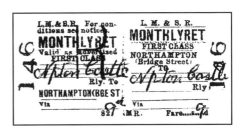

EAST OF NORTHAMPTON

9. This crossing box was open from 1900 until 21st August 1966 when this part of the line closed. The crossing keeper had to swing each gate individually, the locking catches being above the targets. (R.J.Essery/R.S.Carpenter)

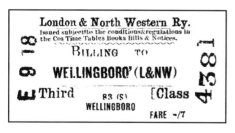

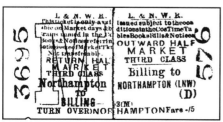

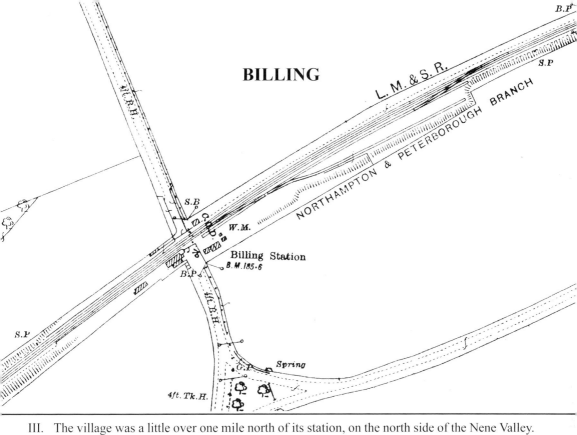

BILLING

III. The village was a little over one mile north of its station, on the north side of the Nene Valley. The population of the adjacent villages, Great and Little Billing, was 356 in 1901.

10. The station opened a few months after the line, on 10th December 1845. We are looking towards Northampton in the 1930s. The name was Billing Road until 1st April 1883. (LOSA)

11.   Seen on 18th July 1958, the structures are in ruins as passenger service had been withdrawn here on 6th October 1952. Only the chimney pots of the station house are visible. (H.C.Casserley)

12.   A lady arrives from the village on 24th April 1961, presumably to watch the shunting in the goods yard, as this did not close until 1st June 1964. The station house still stood in 2016. (B.W.L.Brooksbank)

13. Pictured on 2nd October 1965 is the 1908 box, which was in use until 21st August 1966, when the route closed between Hardingstone Junction and Wellingborough London Road Level Crossing. (R.J.Essery/R.S.Carpenter)

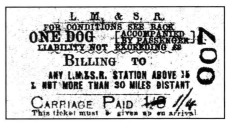

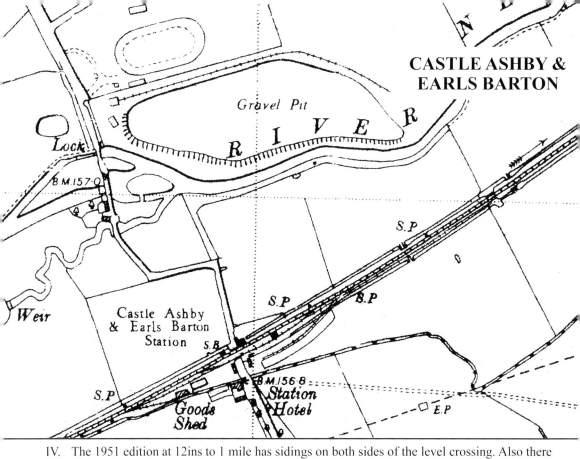

CASTLE ASHBY & EARLS BARTON

IV. The 1951 edition at 12ins to 1 mile has sidings on both sides of the level crossing. Also there is a railway close to the gravel pit. The lock is one of many that make the River Nene navigable. In 1901, Castle Ashby housed 256 and Earls Barton 2914.

14. A train bound for Peterborough arrives on 13th April 1936, hauled by class 1P 2-4-2T no. 6699. This successful class numbered around 160, the first one being seen in 1890. A successful cottage industry in Earls Barton had been boot and shoe making; small workshops developed from this. (H.F.Wheeller/R.S.Carpenter)

15.   No. 44521 was an 0-6-0 classified 4F, one of a batch of 580 introduced by the LMS in 1924. It is destined for Northampton and is almost level with the small cattle dock. Both village centres were about 1¼ miles from the station. (SLS coll.)

16.   Taken from a departing train on 29th April 1953, this photograph includes the canopy of the goods shed and the gates being reopened to road traffic, by hand. On the right are two cattle wagons. (H.C.Casserley)

17.   A closer record of the gates on 4th July 1959 includes one of the two wicket gates, which allowed people to cross the tracks under supervision, when the main gates were closed. Many would enjoy the intricacies of point rodding and signal wiring. (R.M.Casserley)

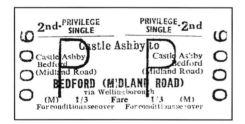

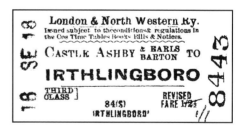

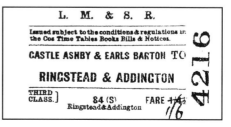

18. The 12.50 Peterborough East to Northampton Castle called at all stations and is seen on the same day. The locomotive is no. 44518, a class 4F 0-6-0, ex-LMS. The main line had been single track for about its first year after opening. (H.C.Casserley)

19. A horse box stands at the cattle dock in about 1960. Very close to it is a paraffin lamp and on the opposite platform is the roofless area for gentlemen. The essential fire buckets adorn the end wall. Further on was Hardwater Crossing, which received half barriers on 19th July 1964. (LOSA)

20.   The 1878 signal box had 36 levers and was in use until 21st August 1966. BR class 9F 2-10-0 no. 92127 is working an up mineral train on 17th April 1961. The provision of an extra pair of gates on a line to link sidings was unusual; we have found only a few cases in over 400 albums. (Milepost 92½)

21.   The former goods shed was built in 1858 and was converted and extended for use as a restaurant called Dunkleys in 1984. It is seen here in 1993, with a protruding coach. The two carriages were used as cocktail and coffee lounges. There were plans for a residential development following the restaurant's closure in 2013. (B.W.L.Brooksbank)

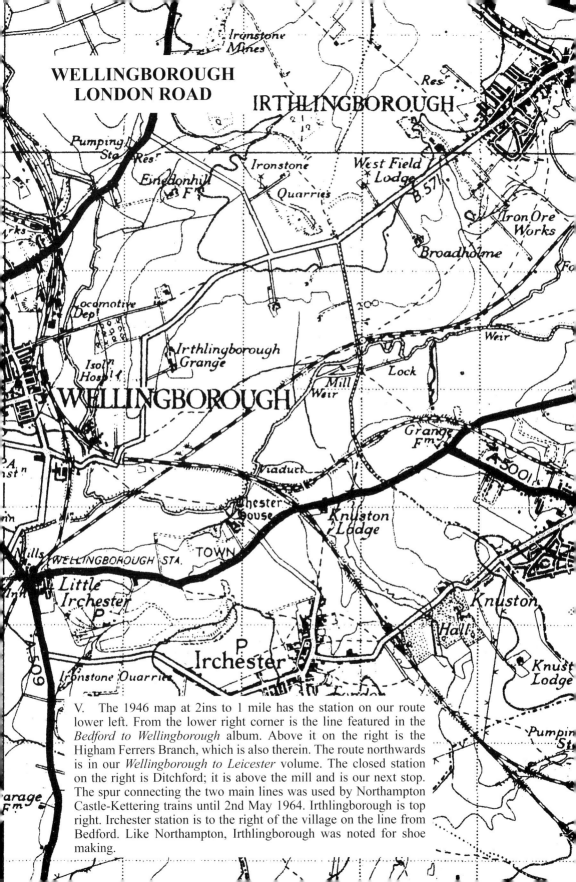

WELLINGBOROUGH
LONDON ROAD

IRTHLINGBOROUGH

Ironstone Mines

Res.

Pumping Sta. Res.

Ironstone Quarries

West Field Lodge

Finedonhill Fm

B.571

Iron Ore Works

Broadholme

Locomotive Dept.

Irthlingborough Grange

Isol'n Hosp.

WELLINGBOROUGH

Mill Weir

Lock

Weir

Grange Fm

A.500

Viaduct

Chester House

Knuston Lodge

WELLINGBOROUGH STA.   TOWN

Mills

Little Irchester

Knuston

Hall

Knust Lodge

A.60

Irchester

P

Ironstone Quarries

Pumping Sta.

arage Fm

V.   The 1946 map at 2ins to 1 mile has the station on our route lower left. From the lower right corner is the line featured in the *Bedford to Wellingborough* album. Above it on the right is the Higham Ferrers Branch, which is also therein. The route northwards is in our *Wellingborough to Leicester* volume. The closed station on the right is Ditchford; it is above the mill and is our next stop. The spur connecting the two main lines was used by Northampton Castle-Kettering trains until 2nd May 1964. Irthlingborough is top right. Irchester station is to the right of the village on the line from Bedford. Like Northampton, Irthlingborough was noted for shoe making.

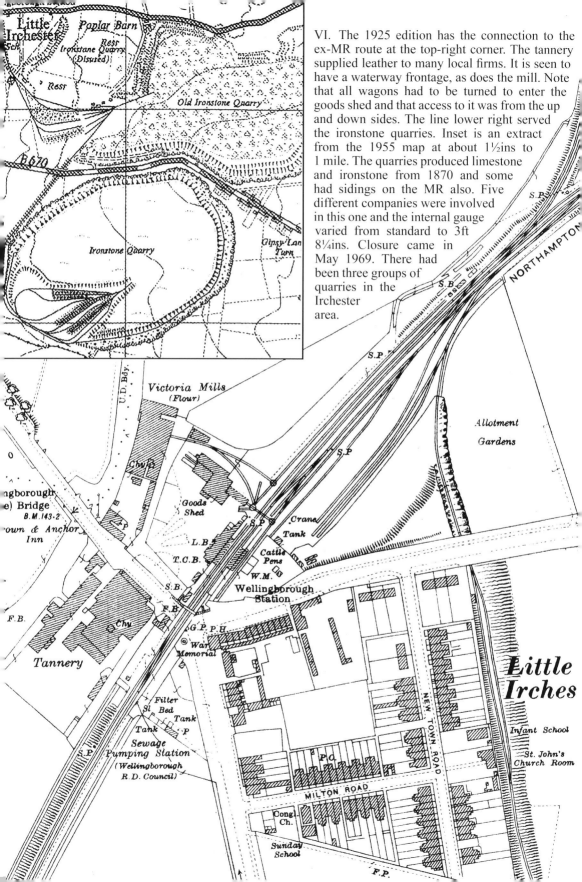

VI. The 1925 edition has the connection to the ex-MR route at the top-right corner. The tannery supplied leather to many local firms. It is seen to have a waterway frontage, as does the mill. Note that all wagons had to be turned to enter the goods shed and that access to it was from the up and down sides. The line lower right served the ironstone quarries. Inset is an extract from the 1955 map at about 1½ins to 1 mile. The quarries produced limestone and ironstone from 1870 and some had sidings on the MR also. Five different companies were involved in this one and the internal gauge varied from standard to 3ft 8¼ins. Closure came in May 1969. There had been three groups of quarries in the Irchester area.

22. The suffix "London Road" was added on 2nd June 1924 and used until closure on 4th May 1964. The MR station became "Midland Road", in that period, and is still in use. The population grew from around 18,000 in 1901 to over 34,000 by 1961. The view is from around 1906. (P.Laming coll.)

23. Class 4F 0-6-0 no. 4512 is approaching the station from the north on 13th April 1936 and is passing life-expired track components. This was the era of wagons which carried their owner's names. Junction Box is in the background. (H.F.Wheeller/R.S.Carpenter)

24. It is 29th April 1953 and we can enjoy the view from the rear of a train departing for Northampton. The porcelain insulators for the telegraph wires were extremely numerous here, each serving a separate circuit. The war memorial is on the right. (H.C.Casserley)

25.   The driver is nearest to us as the push-pull unit is propelled towards us. Only the fireman remained on the engine in this direction on this economical system used for local trains. This is on a service to Northampton Castle from Wellingborough Midland Road, known to the staff as the "Wellingborough Motor". The line to the flour mill is on the left. (LOSA)

26.   Another view from around 1960 and this is southwards. Many architects avoided having stanchions obstructing the platforms, but here they are adorned with four brackets each. (LOSA)

27. The spur to Midland Road station curves to the left, near the signal post. The private siding to Little Irchester Ironstone Quarries was served by the furthest curve on the right. This is Junction Box, which had 30 levers, the frame coming into use in December 1911. (Milepost 92½)

28. A northward panorama from the footbridge on 11th April 1964 includes class 5 4-6-0 no. 44682 with a train from Peterborough. The class was introduced in 1934, but this was one of a batch with roller bearings, started in 1950. (E. Wilmshurst)

29. The goods yard had a 10-ton crane and closed on 7th November 1966, with the line. It is seen soon after, with netting across the track. The 1886 signal box had a 25-lever frame and carries the words LONDON ROAD. (Milepost 92½)

30. The fine frontage was recorded not long after closure. An action committee to retain the line called a campaign meeting, but raised just £1-18s-3d, almost £2. The high-level dual carriageway of the A45 now runs across the site. (R.J.Essery/R.S.Carpenter)

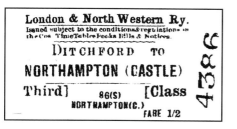

London & North Western Ry.
Issued subject to the conditions & regulations in
the Cos TimeTable Books Bills & Notices.
DITCHFORD   TO
NORTHAMPTON (CASTLE)
Third]   86(S)   [Class
NORTHAMPTON(C.)
FARE 1/2
4386

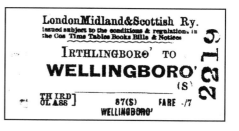

LondonMidland&Scottish Ry.
Issued subject to the conditions & regulations in
the Cos Time Tables Books Bills & Notices
IRTHLINGBORO' TO
WELLINGBORO'
(S)
THIRD
CLASS]   87(S)   FARE -/7
WELLINGBORO'
2215

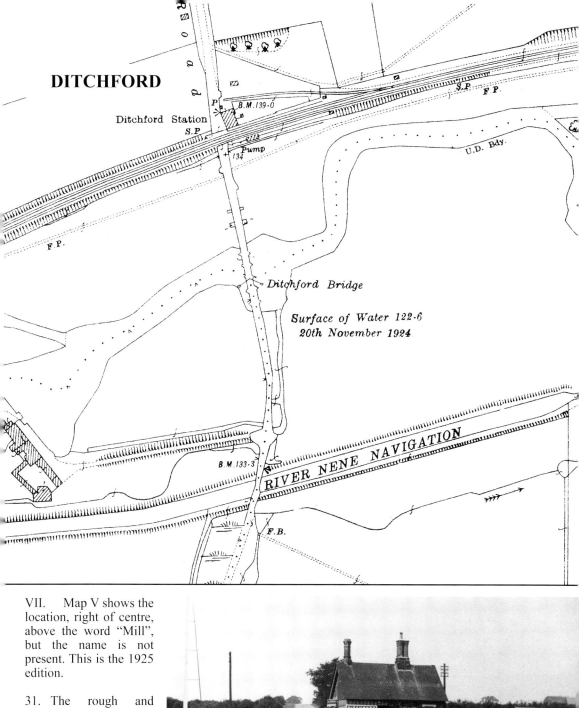

DITCHFORD

Ditchford Station

B.M.139·0

S.P.

Pump

134

F.P.

S.P.

F.P.

U.D. Bdy.

Ditchford Bridge

Surface of Water 122·6
20th November 1924

F.P.

B.M.133·3

RIVER NENE NAVIGATION

F.B.

VII. Map V shows the location, right of centre, above the word "Mill", but the name is not present. This is the 1925 edition.

31. The rough and dung-loaded road was deemed suitable for a postcard. Both buildings are marked on the map, along with the single short siding. (P.Laming coll.)

32. Two photos from 11th May 1962 complete our survey of this little used station. It closed to passengers as early as 1st November 1924, although it could be used by railway staff and families until about 1952. Class 5 4-6-0 no. 45392 is heading for Peterborough with freight. The photographer's 1935 Morris 12 is present. (H.C.Casserley)

33. The goods yard had closed on 15th May 1950, but both platforms had remained fairly intact. The two signals were worked by the gate keeper from an eight-lever ground frame. There is now no trace of the station. (H.C.Casserley)

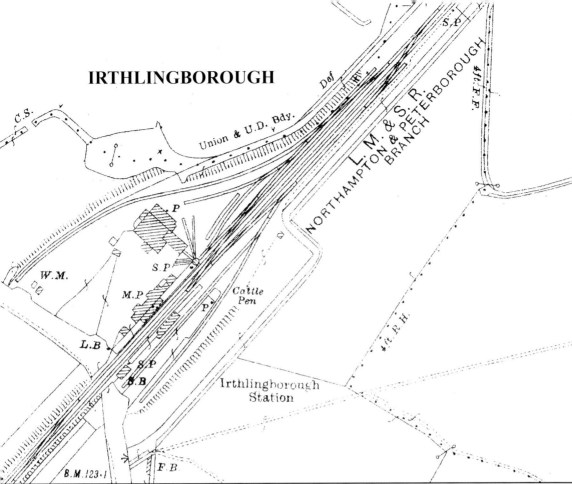

IRTHLINGBOROUGH

VIII.   The mines and quarries are shown just below the town, around the top right of map V. This is the 1926 edition. The station opened as HIGHAM FERRARS with the line and became HIGHAM FERRERS in 1852. It was HIGHAM FERRERS & IRTHLINGBOROUGH on 28th April 1885 and just IRTHLINGBOROUGH from 1st October 1910.

34.   We are on the bridge over the Nene Navigation, which is just beyond the left border of the map. The siding on the left of it is carrying the coal wagons standing on the left of this picture. The post mark is 1910. (P.Laming coll.)

35.   The lofty signal box was opened in February 1887 and was fitted with 25 levers. It closed with the line on 6th June 1966. Further west was Irthlingborough Iron Ore Co's Siding Box, which opened in November 1890, with 16 levers. A bridge for the A6 was built in the background, not long before closure. (P.Laming coll.)

36.   A view from about 1912 features the single-storey extension carrying the sign LADIES. The flight of three steps was movable and were used to help the immobile into and out of trains. The town housed 4314 in 1901 and 5200 in 1961. (LOSA)

37.   A train for Peterborough is departing in February 1947, while we examine the additional hardware needed for gates remotely operated by a wheel in the signal box. (W.A.Camwell/SLS)

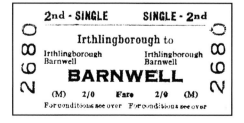

38.　　Class 4F 0-6-0 no. 44491 is calling with the 12.30 Peterborough East to Northampton Castle on 30th April 1960. Coal hoppers stand in the goods yard, which was open until 6th June 1966. The lines on the right served the cattle pens. (H.C.Casserley)

39.　　The fine building from 1876 is seen on 11th April 1964. Sadly, it was demolished in 1970. It had closed to passengers on 4th May 1964. The platforms were still in place in 1975. By the 21st century, gravel in large quantities crossed the road here, in an overhead enclosed conveyor. All traces of the station were lost. (E.Wilmshurst)

West of Irthlingborough

40. It is 12th April 1938 and we are near to the entrance to Irthlingborough Mines, also the approach to the bunker serving the rank of kilns, originally used for calcining by Ebbw Vale Steel. A Ruston & Hornsby locomotive stands at the head of a loaded train. Note overhead cables for the four trolley locomotives working here. Ebbw Vale Steel leased the site in 1915 and laid the 3ft gauge tramway. One of the two Ruston & Hornsby diesel locomotives is seen. (Ruston & Hornsby)

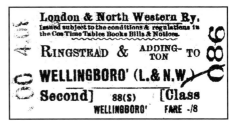

41. A Nordberg 'Trackshifter' is being used to recover rail during lifting operations with a chain at Irchester Quarries on 24th August 1969. This was not an unusual operation, as the working faces moved frequently. Nearby was a cement works and the Metropolitan Brick & Tile Company. (S.A.Leleux)

42. Seldom seen in daylight was this battery electric locomotive. It was built by Greenwood & Batley in 1938 and the power was stored in its tender, seen on 21st May 1964. There was a fleet of 560 wagons at its maximum and closure came in 1966. (S.A.Leleux)

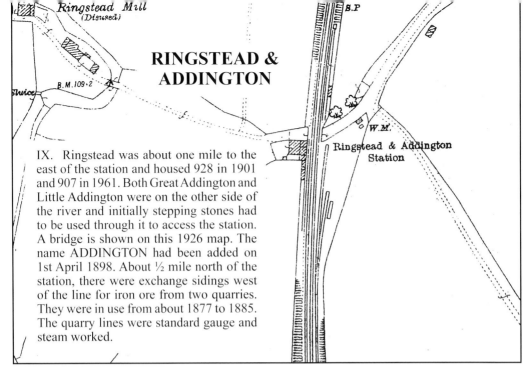

RINGSTEAD & ADDINGTON

IX. Ringstead was about one mile to the east of the station and housed 928 in 1901 and 907 in 1961. Both Great Addington and Little Addington were on the other side of the river and initially stepping stones had to be used through it to access the station. A bridge is shown on this 1926 map. The name ADDINGTON had been added on 1st April 1898. About ½ mile north of the station, there were exchange sidings west of the line for iron ore from two quarries. They were in use from about 1877 to 1885. The quarry lines were standard gauge and steam worked.

43.   A northward panorama from about 1950 includes the LMS style Hawkseye running-in board and the gate to the goods yard. Just beyond the signal was a cast iron urinal, at the foot of the platform ramp. An 8-lever ground frame was provided in the open on the right platform from 1887. (W.A.Camwell/SLS)

44.   The details were recorded on 29th April 1954, 10 years before passenger service ceased. The goods yard was in use until 7th August 1967. The weighbridge office is on the right and marked W.M. for Weighing Machine on the map. The main buildings have long gone and there are now no traces. Butlin Bevan & Co. loaded iron ore here between about 1871 and 1891. The quarry was east of the station and horses hauled around 1000 tons along the road each weekday. (H.C.Casserley)

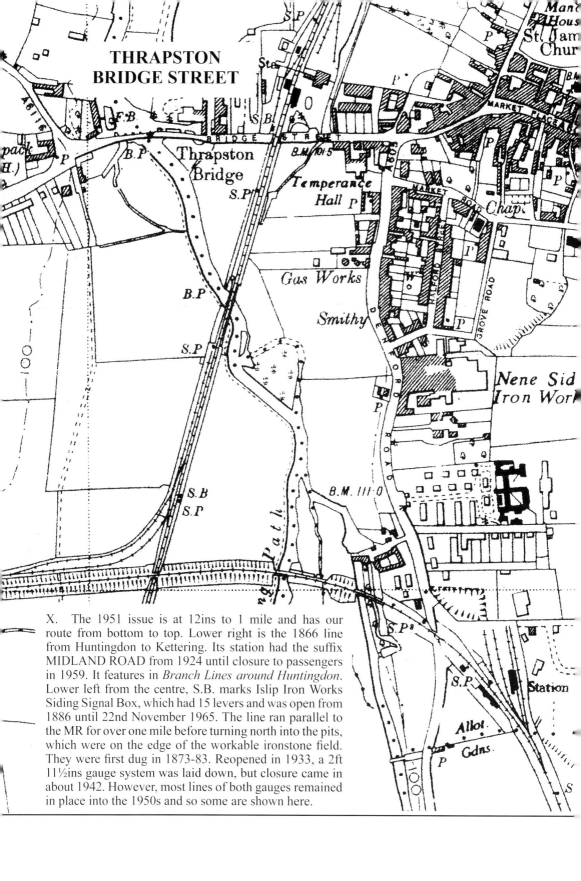

**THRAPSTON
BRIDGE STREET**

X. The 1951 issue is at 12ins to 1 mile and has our route from bottom to top. Lower right is the 1866 line from Huntingdon to Kettering. Its station had the suffix MIDLAND ROAD from 1924 until closure to passengers in 1959. It features in *Branch Lines around Huntingdon*. Lower left from the centre, S.B. marks Islip Iron Works Siding Signal Box, which had 15 levers and was open from 1886 until 22nd November 1965. The line ran parallel to the MR for over one mile before turning north into the pits, which were on the edge of the workable ironstone field. They were first dug in 1873-83. Reopened in 1933, a 2ft 11½ins gauge system was laid down, but closure came in about 1942. However, most lines of both gauges remained in place into the 1950s and so some are shown here.

45. An E was added to the name from 1866 to 1886 and BRIDGE STREET was the suffix from 1867 to 1896 and again from 2nd June 1924, until closure. BOVRIL appeared on most stations and is here close to the tall chimney on the laundry boiler. (P.Laming coll.)

46. It is 8th July 1953 and class D16/3 4-4-0 no. 62535 heads the 3.45pm Peterborough East to Northampton Castle. It had been LNER class D16/2. The population here rose from 1747 in 1901 to 1994 in 1961. (W.A.Camwell/SLS)

47.   The box was opened in 1886, with a 30-lever frame. It remained in use until 22nd November 1965, when the route southwards closed. The line northwards lost all services on 4th May 1964. The photo includes the water tank and is from 29th April 1954. (H.C.Casserley)

48.   We move on to 13th April 1959 and included here is the shielded doorway to the gents, plus most of the cattle dock. The goods yard can be located by the van; there was a 5-ton capacity crane provided. The site was cleared for industrial use. (H.C.Casserley)

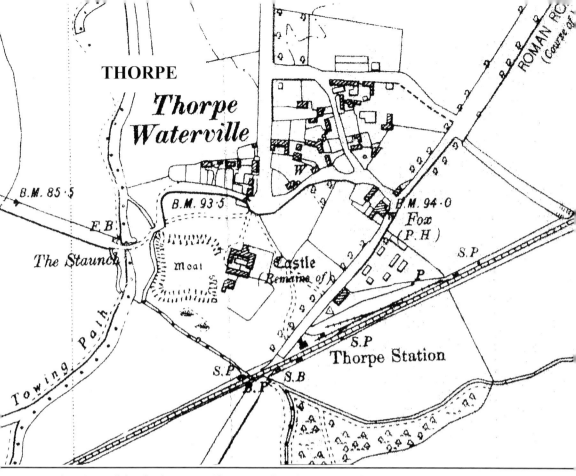

XI. The 1951 edition is shown at 12ins to 1 mile. The tree-lined former Roman Road became the A605 in 1919. The road to the left border continued to the village of Aldwincle, one mile distant.

49. A postcard from 1906 includes a well-covered lady on the foot crossing and part of the gate wheel for the main crossing gates, in the signal box window. The train has goods stock at the back of it and a cart waits near the gate. (P.Laming coll.)

50. A retired van body is acting as a parcels shed, while a horse box stands near the dock. The lorry appears to be from the early 1930s and a loading gauge is in the distance. The boards on the right cover the point rodding and signal wires. (LOSA)

51. The lady has just descended from a train bound for Northampton and is no doubt hearing "Ticket, please". It is 29th September 1954 and the goods yard seems empty. It had no crane and closed with the line on 4th May 1964. The building was not destroyed, but was greatly extended for private use. (R.M.Casserley)

52. It is 22nd April 1959 and we can now see that one gate was sufficient to reach across the main road. The other one had the same great angle to swing. The box was completed in December 1880. (H.C.Casserley)

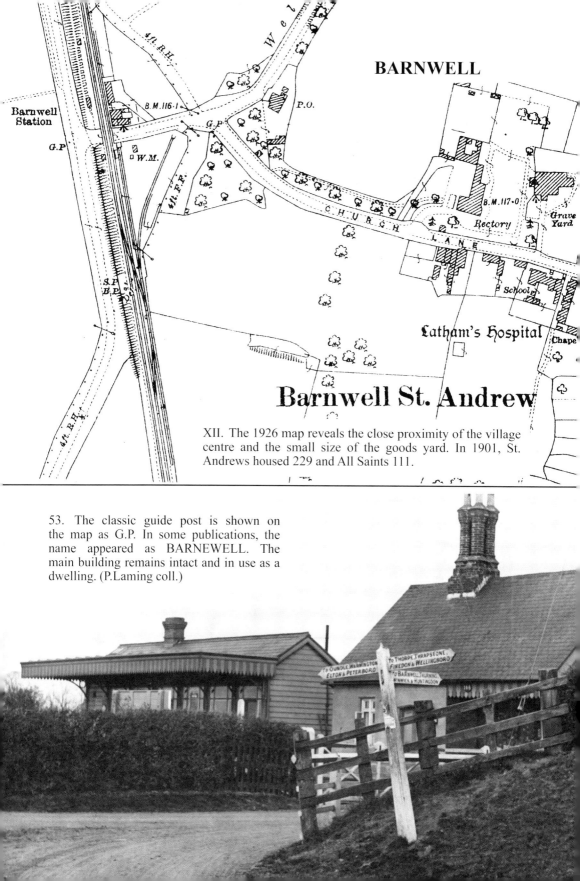

BARNWELL

Barnwell
Station

CHURCH LANE

B.M.117·0

Rectory

Grave
Yard

School

Latham's Hospital

Chape

Barnwell St. Andrew

XII. The 1926 map reveals the close proximity of the village centre and the small size of the goods yard. In 1901, St. Andrews housed 229 and All Saints 111.

53. The classic guide post is shown on the map as G.P. In some publications, the name appeared as BARNEWELL. The main building remains intact and in use as a dwelling. (P.Laming coll.)

54.   Remaining to be seen in the 21st century was the building on the right, together with the adjacent platform face. This view is from April 1954. The LMS extended the down platform in the Autumn of 1943 to accommodate full-length ambulance trains serving Lilford Hall Military Hospital. (R.M.Casserley)

55.   The station was often used by royalty during visits to the nearby estate of the Duke of Gloucester. Two photographs from 22nd April 1959 complete our survey. There was a ground frame near the rodding tunnel under the platform, this controlling the signals. (R.M.Casserley)

56. Royal journeys were probably planned in detail to avoid the use of this small urinal. The residents nearby numbered 452 in 1961. The hook was provided for the oil lamp, which was thus able to illuminate the name board. (H.C.Casserley)

57. Seen in April 1964, the wooden building (left) was moved bodily to Wansford station on a low-loader on 6th April 1977. The tiles and protruding parts were removed first and it has subsequently served as a station shop. Here is another van body serving as a parcel store. The A605 is on the right. (E.Wilmshurst)

OUNDLE

XIII.   The town centre was about ½ mile south of the wharf, which is lower left on this 1926 edition. The name is spoken with the "ow" in "how" by most locals. The public school in the town centre has brought fame and distinction to the area. The crane is shown as Cr. and was rated at 5-ton capacity. The town housed 2404 in 1901 and 3380 in 1961.

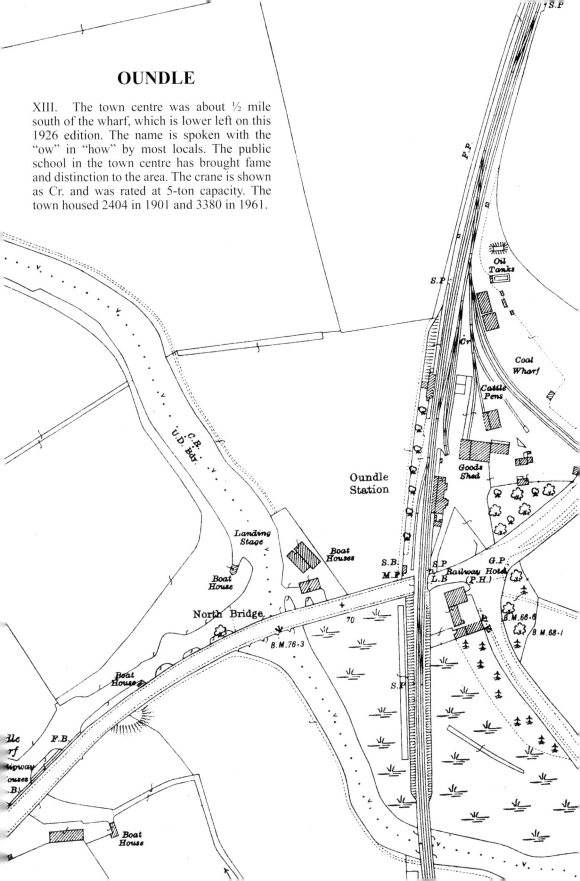

58. Access to the goods shed was then via two wagon turntables, one of which is in the foreground in this postcard view from around 1900. A spur to the running line was behind the camera. The 0-6-0 was known as a "Cauliflower", a type introduced in 1880. (P.Laming coll.)

PETERBOROUGH, WELLINGBOROUGH and NORTHAMPTON

Miles		am		am		am		pm		pm		pm		pm		pm				
								Week Days only													
—	Peterborough (East) .. dep	6 43	..	7 35	..	9 46	..	12 30		12 40		3 50	..	6 0	..	8 49		..	..	..	..
13½	Oundle	7 5	....	7 56	...	10 7	....	12 51		1 1	....	4 11	....	6 21	....	9 10	....	....			
15½	Barnwell	7 10	..	8 1	...	10 12	..	12 56		1 6		4 16	..	6 26	..	9 15	....	..			
19	Thorpe	7 16	..	8 7	...	10 18	....	1 2		1 12		4 22	..	6 32	....	9 21	....	..			
21½	Thrapston (Bridge Street) ..	7 23	..	8 12	...	10 24	..	1 8		1 18	..	4 29	..	6 40	..	9 27	....	..			
24½	Ringstead & Addington	7 29	...	8 18	....	10 30	..	1 14		1 24	....	4 35	....	6 46	....	9 33	....	..			
27½	Irthlingborough..	7 36	...	8 24	...	10 36	..	1 22		1 32	..	4 44	..	6 52	....	9 39	....	..			
31½	Wellingborough (London Rd.)	7 45	..	8 34	...	10 45	...	1 31		1 41	....	4 54	..	7C 5	..	9 47	....	..			
35½	Castle Ashby & Earls Barton ..	7 53	..	8 42	...	10 53	..	1 39		1 49		5 2	..		....		....	..			
42½	Northampton (Bridge St.)...	8 5	..	8 54	..	11 5	....	1 51		2 1	....		....	7 23	....	10 5	....	..			
43½	,, (Castle) .. arr	8 9	..	8 58	..	11 9	..	1 55		2 5	..	5 17	..	7 27	..	10 11	..	..			

(Saturdays only · Except Saturdays · Saturdays only)

Miles		am		am		pm		pm		pm		pm					
								Week Days only									
—	Northampton (Castle) .. dep	7 13	..	9 28	..	12 28	..		..	5 10	..	6 42	..	..	..	..	..
1	,, (Bridge St.) ...	7 17	..	9 31	...	12 31	..		..	5 13	..	6 45	..	..	..		
8	Castle Ashby & Earls Barton ..	7 28	...	9 42	..	12 42	..			5 24	..	6 56	..	..	..		
12	Wellingborough (London Rd.)	7 37	....	9 50	..	12 51	....	4 21		5 35	..	7 7	..	..	..		
16½	Irthlingborough..	7 46	....	9 58	..	12 59	..	4 28		5 43	....	7 15	..	..	..		
19	Ringstead & Addington	7 52	....		...	1 5	..	4 34		5 49	..	7 21	..	..	..		
22½	Thrapston (Bridge Street) ..	7 59	..	10 8	..	1 12	..	4 42		5 58	..	7 28	..	..	..		
24½	Thorpe	8 6	..	10 15	..	1 19	..	4 49		6 5	..	7 35	..	..	..		
28	Barnwell	8 12	..	10 21	..	1 25	..	4 55		6 11	..	7 41	..	..	..		
30½	Oundle	8 19	..	10 27	..	1 31	..	5 0		6 17	..	7 47	..	..	..		
43½	Peterborough (East) .. arr	8 38	..	10 46	..	1 50	..		..	6 38	..	8 6	..	..	..		

(Except Saturdays and not during school holiday periods (A) · Saturdays only)

A For dates see supplements to timetable
C Arrives Wellingborough (London Rd.) 7 0 pm

September 1962

59. The goods shed is on the right and well spaced from the main building - see map XIII. The staggering of the platforms is clear in this view from the same early era. A "Cauliflower" is arriving. (P.Laming coll.)

60. The foot crossing is between the ends of both trains and is clear in picture 63. The gate keeper had a good cabin (right), complete with a stove. It later became the lamp room and oil store. (SLS coll.)

61.	The siding on the left formed the goods yard in the early years and later became a refuge siding. The main yard is beyond the water column in this panorama from the 1930s. The canopy was removed after closure and the building adapted for residential use. It is now surrounded by new homes. (LOSA)

62.	The 1887 signal box stands opposite the earlier accommodation for the gate keeper. Passenger service was withdrawn on 4th May 1964. This photo was taken from a DMU hired as a farewell special on 4th November 1972. (H.C.Casserley)

63.   Goods traffic ceased here on 6th November 1972, along with specials for Oundle School at the start and end of term. The up platform had two sack trucks when photographed on 22nd April 1959. (H.C.Casserley)

64.   The short cattle dock is visible through the railings on 11th April 1964, as class 6P5F 2-6-0 no. 42945 runs in bound for Northampton Castle. Built in 1933, it was the first of its class. The main building forms a fine dwelling in 2016; "the finest" according to Mr. John Betjeman. (E.Wilmshurst)

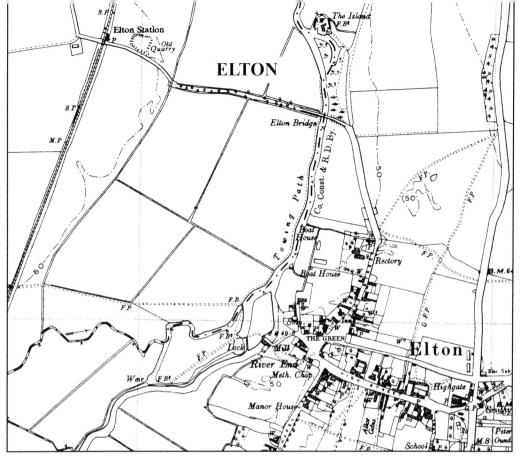

XIV. The 1951 edition is at 6ins to 1 mile and includes the dots and dashes of the boundary between Northamptonshire and Huntingdonshire along the River Nene. There were 674 residents in 1901 and 550 listed in 1961. More quarries had been dug earlier, south of the one shown.

65. A southward view from the 1930s features three small buildings and a urinal on the opposite platform. The station opened on 2nd October 1846, but only had one siding. (LOSA)

66.   The staff residence and the parcels shed are seen on 23rd June 1959. The latter often stored locally made Vinko pedal cycles. Services had ceased here on 7th December 1953. A ground frame on the up platform controlled the signals; it closed on 10th August 1952. Access to the siding and weighing machine was through the gate on the left. The site was later cleared. (H.C.Casserley)

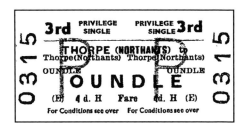

Views of the route hereon subsequent to the NVR takeover in 1977 are to be found in pictures 103 to 118 herein.

67.   We arrive on the line on the left at Yarwell Junction, the route to Seaton being on the right. This line and the box opened on 1st November 1879. The photograph is from 12th April 1966. (Milepost 92½)

68.   We look east on the same day towards the limestone ridge, through which the line runs in Wansford Tunnel. The box had 20 levers and closed on 1st January 1967. The line from Nassington came to an end in 1971 and from Oundle in 1972. From 1967 until those dates, the tracks were worked as two single lines, with staffs to allow one engine on each, these being issued from Wansford signal box. (Milepost 92½)

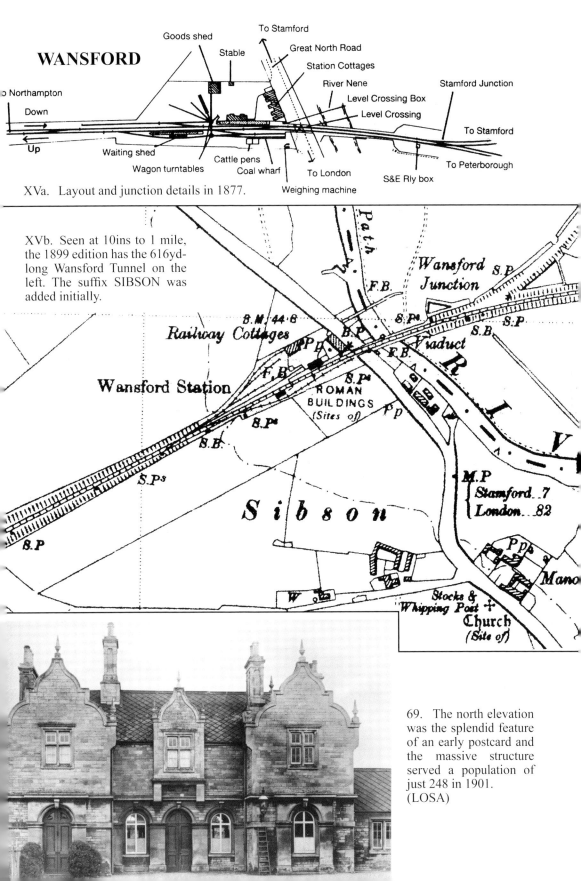

WANSFORD

To Northampton
Down

Up

Goods shed
Stable
To Stamford
Great North Road
Station Cottages
River Nene
Level Crossing Box
Level Crossing
Stamford Junction
To Stamford
To Peterborough
Waiting shed
Cattle pens
Wagon turntables
Coal wharf
To London
S&E Rly box
Weighing machine

XVa. Layout and junction details in 1877.

XVb. Seen at 10ins to 1 mile, the 1899 edition has the 616yd-long Wansford Tunnel on the left. The suffix SIBSON was added initially.

69. The north elevation was the splendid feature of an early postcard and the massive structure served a population of just 248 in 1901. (LOSA)

70. The main building is left of centre and the facilities for cattle are on the left. Both canopies can be studied in this view from around 1910, as can the staggering of the platforms. (LOSA)

71. This photo from about 1930 enables us to see through Wansford Tunnel and enjoy several of the oil lamps. The connections allowed access to the goods yard from both running lines. (LOSA)

72. A Northampton Castle to Peterborough East train is approaching the level crossing around 1950, hauled by class D16/3 4-4-0 no. 62535. Passenger service ceased here on 1st July 1957. (W.A.Camwell/SLS)

73. Stamford trains used the platform in the lower right corner from 1867 to 1929, the route curving left beyond the distant post. The goods yard closed on 30th July 1964. The 1907 signal box had 60 levers and closed on 30th March 1971, although trains passed until 6th November 1972. (W.A.Camwell/SLS)

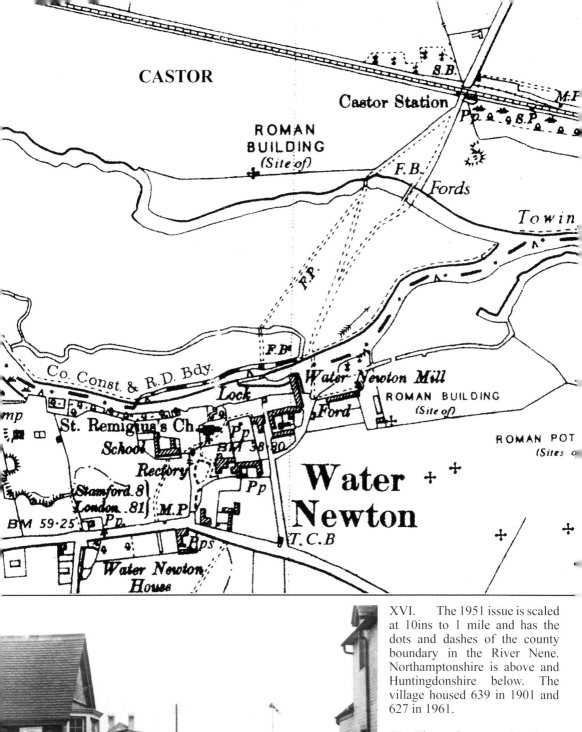

CASTOR

Castor Station

ROMAN
BUILDING
(Site of)

F.B.
Fords

S.B.

M.P

Towin

Co. Const. & R.D. Bdy.

F.B⁴

Water Newton Mill

ROMAN BUILDING
(Site of)

Lock

Ford

ROMAN POT
(Sites o

St. Remigius's Ch.

School

BM 38·30

Rectory

Pp

Water
Newton

Stamford 8
London 81

M.P

BM 59·25

Pp

T.C.B

Water Newton
House

XVI.   The 1951 issue is scaled at 10ins to 1 mile and has the dots and dashes of the county boundary in the River Nene. Northamptonshire is above and Huntingdonshire below. The village housed 639 in 1901 and 627 in 1961.

74.   The station opened in about 1850. We look east in around 1910 and can find the points to the single siding. Goods traffic ceased on 28th December 1964, but passengers were not welcome after 1st July 1957. (LOSA)

ORTON WATERVILLE

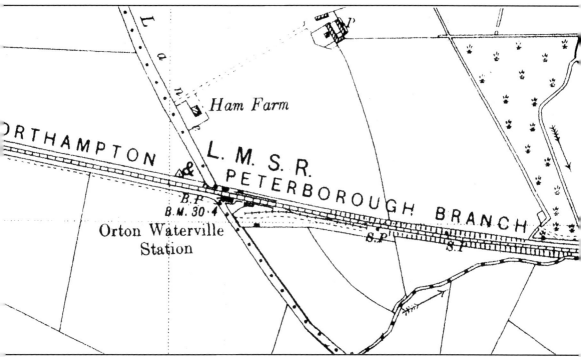

XVII.   The 1938 edition at 12ins to 1 mile shows the loop and sidings for goods traffic. The name used was OVERTON until 1st August 1913. The station served 276 souls in 1901.

75.   This is the view towards Wansford in about 1900 and features the signal box, which was opened with the line, but rebuilt in February 1878. Its lower half and the house opposite were brick built. (P.Laming coll.)

76. Apart from one fire bucket missing, all looks well in this photo from the 1930s. The loading gauge is evident, but there was no crane. Gardening proceeds on the right. The later Ferry Meadows station was situated a little to the east of this one. (LOSA)

77. A westward panorama from 7th May 1960 includes undergrowth, as the last passenger had left on 5th October 1942. However, railwaymen and their families were allowed to travel from here until about June 1962. Goods traffic ceased here on 28th December 1964. The box closed on 13th June 1966; its gate wheel is evident. (R.M.Casserley coll.)

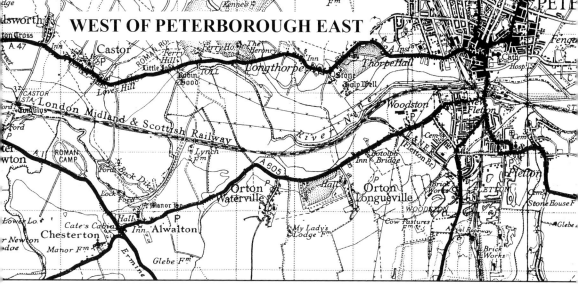

WEST OF PETERBOROUGH EAST

XVIII.   The 1946 edition at 1 ins to 1 mile includes a Roman site southeast of Castor station and the Fletton Branch, which was in use from April 1881. After 1914, it was used mainly for freight and had a connection to the Fletton Brickworks lines. Some of these can be seen with a lens or enjoyed larger in the *Hitchin to Peterborough* album. The loop was in use until October 1929, but was reopened in December 1947. Closed again in November 1965, it was restored in 1974 to facilitate the transfer of stock to and from the NVR. At its west end is Longville Junction, which had a signal box from 1880 until 1929, after which a ground frame sufficed. There were sidings between the diverging routes that served the British Sugar Corporation, from 1928 until February 1991.

78.   Peterborough East is shown as a black rectangle above the "n" of New Fletton on the map and the line on the right of it is the LNER route from March. We are looking west from the bridge over it on 7th April 1953 as a D6 class 4-4-0 runs tender first to East station. On the left is an A3 at the head of an express bound for King's Cross. The lattice girders had replaced a wooden structure in 1896. The bridge was doubled in width in 1922-24 to take four tracks. Fletton Road Junction signal box had been completed here in June 1900 and its 80-lever frame was in use until 1932. East Box was then in control. It is to be seen in picture 87. (LOSA)

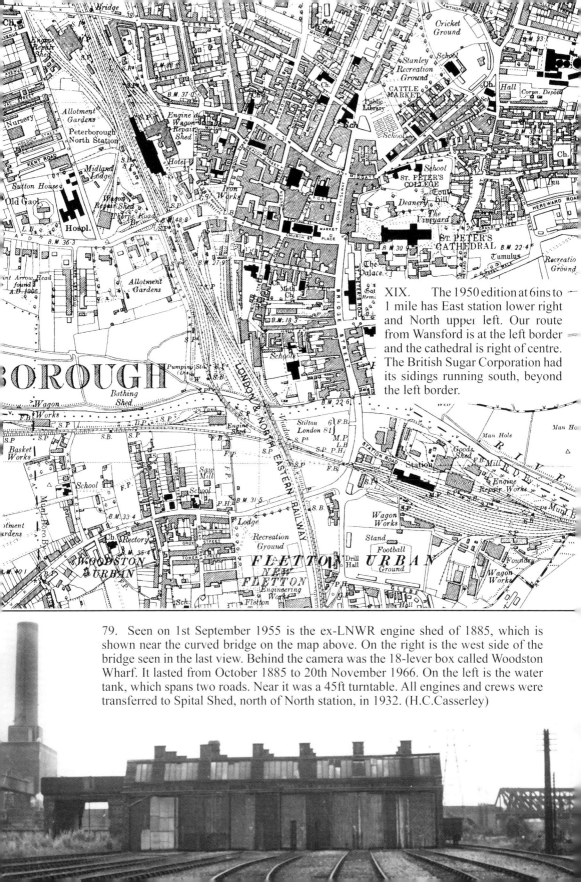

XIX.   The 1950 edition at 6ins to 1 mile has East station lower right and North upper left. Our route from Wansford is at the left border and the cathedral is right of centre. The British Sugar Corporation had its sidings running south, beyond the left border.

79.   Seen on 1st September 1955 is the ex-LNWR engine shed of 1885, which is shown near the curved bridge on the map above. On the right is the west side of the bridge seen in the last view. Behind the camera was the 18-lever box called Woodston Wharf. It lasted from October 1885 to 20th November 1966. On the left is the water tank, which spans two roads. Near it was a 45ft turntable. All engines and crews were transferred to Spital Shed, north of North station, in 1932. (H.C.Casserley)

80. The station was GER property by 1862, as was the northern track as far as the bridge seen in picture 78. The first user of the site was the L&BR, the Eastern Counties Railway running in from 14th January 1847. (P.Laming coll.)

81. It is a rare postcard that shows a train standing at two platforms at once. The arrangement shows more clearly in picture 85. The locomotive appears to be no. 715. It is a GER class T19. (P.Laming coll.)

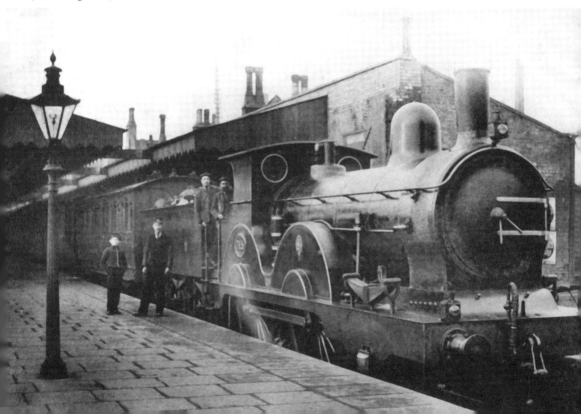

PETERBOROUGH EAST

82. The suffix EAST was added on 1st July 1923. Part of the footbridge over the single track is evident beyond the steam, on 29th May 1937. (H.C.Casserley)

83. It is 20th May 1938 and a train stands at platforms 1 and 2. This unusual arrangement can still be found at Guildford, but doors can no longer be opened on both sides at once. No. 25319 *Bucephalus* is a 4-4-0 of class 3P, ex-LNWR, and is on the goods line. (H.C.Casserley)

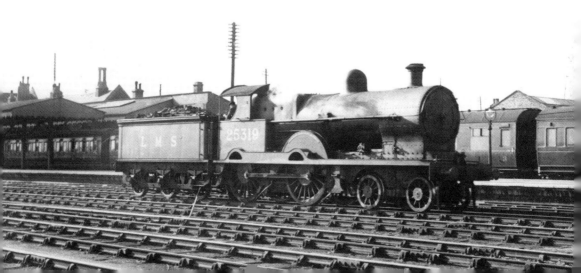

84. East engine shed, goods shed and the adjacent Cadge & Colman flour mill are seen in 1945, along with the cathedral and much of the goods yard. A 60ft turntable was added here in January 1960 for turning Travelling Post Office coaches. The area is now known as Fletton Quays. After 1923, the LNER allocated 38 engines here. (P.Waszak)

85. Ex-LMS class 4F 0-6-0 no. 44519 waits to leave with a train for Northampton, as ex-GNR class C12 4-4-2T no. 67368 stands on the right on 10th April 1954. (J.P.Wilson/Rail Archive Stephenson)

86. The station closed to freight traffic on 17th April 1966 and to passengers on 6th June 1966, but was converted to a parcels depot on 21st September 1970, closing on 23rd December 1970. The historic buildings were subject to an act of official vandalism and destroyed in 1972. However, attitudes change and the engine shed was listed Grade II and acquired for use as the head office of Peterborough City Council in 2012. The engine shed had been used for carriage and wagon repairs from 1939 until the 1970s. (D.K.Jones coll.)

For other views see *Branch Lines around March;* **this also includes** *Peterborough North,* **as does** *Hitchin to Peterborough, Peterborough to Newark, Peterborough to Kings Lynn* **and** *Branch Lines around Wisbech.*

87. A DMU from Cambridge passes through in 1969. The view is from Fletton Road bridge, which had replaced a level crossing on 20th September 1934. One platform edge was still in place in 2016. East Box had 70 levers and was worked from 1932 until 10th June 1973. (A.C.Mott)

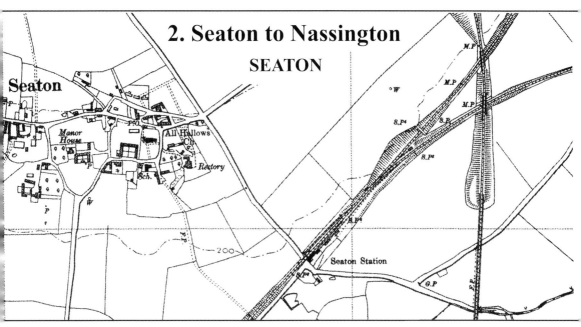

2. Seaton to Nassington

SEATON

XX. The ex-MR route from Kettering to Nottingham is from lower right to the top. Our album carrying those names contains the details. The line to the right border is our route towards Peterborough, while diagonally are the tracks from Rugby to Stamford. This part was in use from 1851 to 1966 and was single track until 1st November 1873, when the line to Wansford opened. This was double from the outset. Subsequently, the route from here to Stamford was regarded as a branch line. Top left is Seaton, which housed 240 in 1901.

88. The first station came into use on 2nd June 1851 and carried the suffix & UPPINGHAM, but this was randomly discontinued. Bradshaw retained it until 1894, when the town received its own branch line, which was operated from here. This panorama is from 22nd August 1953. Class C12 4-4-2T no. 67368 stands on the left with the 11.10 to Uppingham. Arriving with the 10.25 Peterborough to Birmingham train is class 5 4-6-0 no. 44714. (H.C.Casserley)

89. This closer view of the north end is from 6th August 1956 and includes two short armed signals used for shunting purposes. The signal box opened in April 1879 and had 48 levers. Closure came on 6th June 1966, with the end of all three routes in this area. (Milepost 92½)

90. It is 14th April 1957 and the Railway Enthusiasts Club ran the "Charnwood Forester". No. 67357 was a class C12 4-4-2T of GNR origin and was used on part of the tour, which was based at King's Cross. It included Ramsey North, Peterborough North, Stamford, Kirby Muxloe, Nuneaton and Kettering. The footbridge was still standing in 2016. (H.C.Casserley)

91. There were three other stations in England with the same name and four more with suffixes. The Casserley touring aid was a 1934 Austin 10, which is centre stage on 21st April 1958. We are looking southwest, with the latest TV aerial evident. (H.C.Casserley)

92.   Bound for Peterborough on 28th March 1959 is a DMU devoid of a yellow front, soon to be mandatory. Just arrived is the connection from Uppingham, hauled by class 3P 4-4-2T no. 41975 (T.G.Hepburn/Rail Archive Stephenson)

93.   Seen on the same day is ex-LMS class 4F 0-6-0 no. 44097. It is taking water before leaving for Peterborough. Freight service started on 21st July 1879 and was discontinued on 6th April 1964. (T.G.Hepburn/Rail Archive Stephenson)

94.   The former MR viaduct is in the background of this eastward panorama from 2nd April 1960. It came into use in 1879 and still carries trains between Corby and Oakham. Two coaches for Uppingham wait in the bay platform. (J.Langford)

95.   The Peterborough lines are on the right and the Stamford ones on the left in this photograph of the remains of the engine shed on 28th August 1960. The signals for trains from Uppingham are on the far left. (R.S.Carpenter)

96. "Jubilee" class 4-6-0 no. 45642 *Boscawen* has just arrived with a Peterborough to Rugby stopping train on 30th April 1963. Passengers have a close encounter with its smoke. (T.G.Hepburn/Rail Archive Stephenson)

WAKERLEY & BARROWDEN

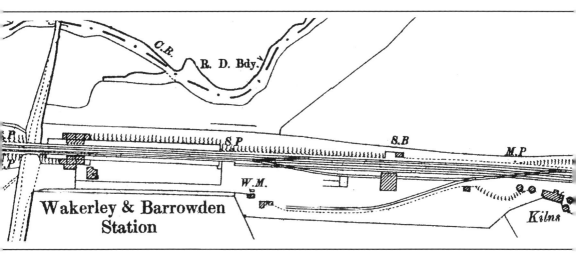

XXI. The 1899 edition is shown at 20ins to 1 mile. Wakerley had 149 residents in 1901 and was close to the south side of the station. Barrowden housed 440 and was almost a mile to the northwest, but they were in different counties. The route west of here is now part of the Jurassic Way.

97. Looking west in around 1900, we find the 1879 signal box in the distance. It lasted until May 1965; the goods yard closed on 28th December 1964 and the station followed on 6th June 1966. Right of centre is the goods shed, which had a 30cwt crane and Monckton's private siding was a mile beyond it from 1881 to about 1931. To the west of the station, there were sidings south of the line serving iron ore quarries of the Partington Steel & Iron Company. They had 2ft 6ins gauge track in use from about 1913 to 1921, using two 0-4-0STs. (P.Laming coll.)

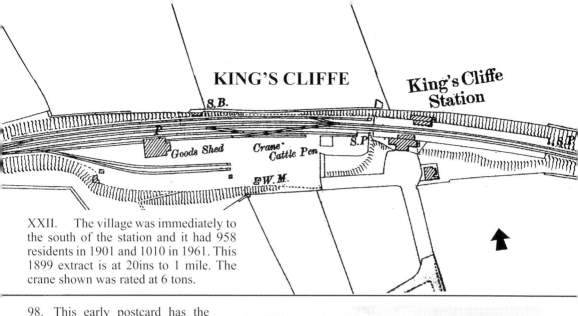

KING'S CLIFFE

King's Cliffe Station

S.B.

Goods Shed

Crane *Cattle Pen*

S.P

E.W.M.

XXII. The village was immediately to the south of the station and it had 958 residents in 1901 and 1010 in 1961. This 1899 extract is at 20ins to 1 mile. The crane shown was rated at 6 tons.

98. This early postcard has the signal box in the distance, but the goods shed is obscured by the up building, on the left. Goods traffic ceased on 3rd June 1968. (P.Laming coll.)

99. It is 29th May 1937 and LMS class 1P 0-4-4T no. 1422 is arriving with the 1.20 SO to Peterborough East. Until 1914, the GNR and LNWR provided a choice of stations to travel to in Peterborough. Service ceased on 6th June 1966, but the canopies went much earlier. (H.C.Casserley)

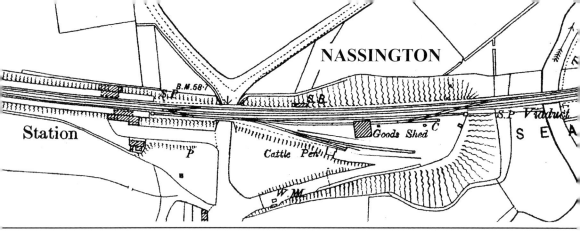

XXIIIa. There were close to 500 residents in 1901-61, the village being on the south side of the station. This is the 1899 edition at 20ins to 1 mile.

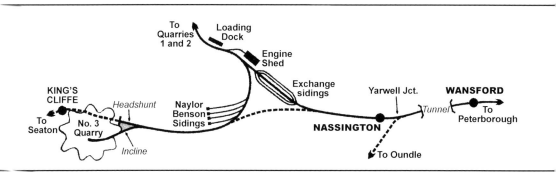

XXIIIb. The quarry system is seen its final form. (The Railway Magazine)

100. The up side building on 9th October 1912 suffered destruction by fire. On the left is the headshunt of the goods yard, which closed on 3rd August 1957. (P.Laming coll.)

101. On the right is the replacement canopy in about 1930. There was a 5-ton crane beyond the goods shed, but traffic ceased on 3rd August 1957. Passenger trains ceased to call on and after 1st July 1957. The bridge over the road is at the end of the platforms. (LOSA)

102. Ex-LMS class 4MT 2-6-4T no. 42573 speeds through with the 12.24 SO Rugby to Peterborough East, on 15th May 1961. The signal box was in use from July 1879 until May 1965. There was a private siding nearby until 26th February 1971; it was used for iron ore and was at the west end of the line in its final years, around one mile west of the station. The quarry was begun in 1939 and there were five exchange sidings served by the standard gauge quarry system. Around 5000 tons per week were often despatched to Scunthorpe and two Hunslet 0-6-0STs did most of the work until closure on 26 February 1971; it had the last steam traction in the industry. Both were preserved. The BR track was lifted in around 1977. (Milepost 92½)

3. Nene Valley Railway

The Peterborough Development Corporation bought the line in 1974. In 1970, the Peterborough Locomotive Society was formed and it soon became the Peterborough Railway Society and then the NVR. Most BR stock had been saved elsewhere and so a collection of European items began. The official opening was on 1st June 1977 and the stock range soon increased.

YARWELL JUNCTION

103. Wansford Tunnel was the western limit of the NVR and the tracks were used for storage, as seen on 4th May 1981. One exception is on the left. It is no. 55002 *The King's Own Yorkshire Light Infantry* with the "Deltic Fenman Tour" from Finsbury Park. BR 4-6-2 no. 70000 *Britannia* of 1951 was resident on the NVR at that time. (T.Heavyside)

104. The tunnel portal was recorded on 29th June 1990 as a JCB flail cutter was about to start work. The remaining track had been used for freight to Oundle until 1972. There had never been a station here. (A.C.Mott)

105. The tracks were realigned in April 2006 to allow for a platform to be built. This view is from 16th April 2011, the station having opened on 7th April 2007. It was a new construction, based on a LNWR design. A travelling post office mail exchange apparatus was later erected as an exhibit of interest. The buffer stops are on the former Seaton line. (P.G.Barnes)

106. The 15.00 from Wansford is seen on the same day, headed by 0-6-0ST Hunslet no. 22. Its works number was 3844 and it has since left the line. Many BR Mk 1 coaches continue in use. A pleasant memorial garden has been created nearby. (P.G.Barnes)

WANSFORD (NVR)

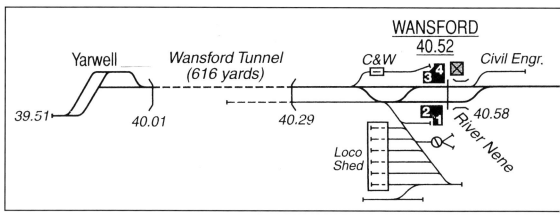

WANSFORD
40.52

107. A panorama from 4th May 1981 features the train described in caption 103 upon its arrival. On the right is ex-Swedish State Railway class S 2-6-2T no. 1178. The yard on the left was occupied by a road transport contractor, while NVR developments were taking place on the right. (T.Heavyside)

XXIV. The track diagram of 2006 shows the original mileage from Blisworth, where the route branched from the London & Birmingham Railway. The figures after the miles are chains. (© TRACKmaps)

108. Seen on 14th August 2008 is the 11.13 Yarwell Junction to Peterborough, hauled by class 5 4-6-0 no. 73050 *City of Peterborough*, built by BR in 1954. The historic tall station building was not available to the NVR until 2016. The building on the left had come from Barnwell station. (P.G.Barnes)

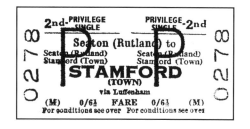

109. The Rolls Royce-engined shunter was no. DL83 and was recorded at work on 16th April 2011. It was built in 1967 and it is waiting to cross the road, which had been the A1, until 1959. (P.G.Barnes)

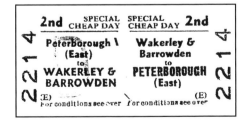

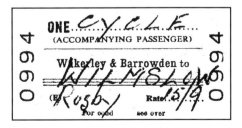

110. On 20th February 2015, demonstration run-pasts were made for a group of photographers. Performing above the River Nene is ex-LNER class D49 4-4-0 no. 62712 *Morayshire*. It had worked from 1928 until 1961. The signal box is described in caption 73. (A.C.Hartless)

111. The NVR headquarters was completed as seen in 1995 and the nearest part formed the book shop. The driver of 0-6-0ST no. 75008 *Swiftsure* was about to respond to the somersault signal on 7th May 2016. The Hunslet Austerity usually ran on the East Lancashire Railway. (V.Mitchell)

FERRY MEADOWS

112. Seen on the same day is the splendid new creation; the canopy had been completed during the previous winter. The building had been the goods office at Fletton Junction, on the GNR main line. It had been purchased for £1, but each brick had to be moved separately. Castor station had not been reopened. (V.Mitchell)

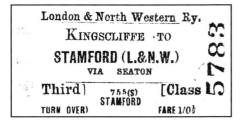

ORTON MERE

113. A loop and temporary building was provided here and no. 70000 was photographed arriving on 4th May 1981, with stock foreign to the line. Here is the eastern entrance to the Nene Park. The station opened in 1977. The signal box came from Maxey Crossing, on the former MR line, north of Peterborough. The station was the terminus of the NVR from 1977-86. (T.Heavyside)

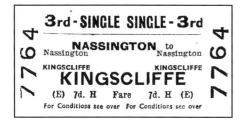

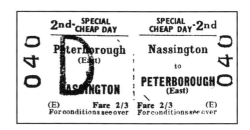

114. As explained earlier, this vast factory produced sugar. Sugar beet arrived by the train load and eventually spare siding space was made available to the NVR. Steam rises as the evidence in this April 1977 panorama. The GNR's Botolph Bridge box was on the right. (P. Waszak)

Mondays to Fridays

Miles			MX	E		G		H ⊠		J							
	BIRMINGHAM NEW STREET	d	..	..		09 05	..	11 33	..	15 58	..	16 04	..	19 38	..	..	..
	RUGBY MIDLAND	d	02 42	06 36	..	09 51	..	13 43	17 00	..	17 28	..	20 52	..	..	..	
	LEICESTER LONDON ROAD	d	02 13	06t40	..	10t02	..	12 45	16 48	..	17 20	..	20 42	..	..	..	
—	MARKET HARBOROUGH	d	03 15	07 15	..	10 27	..	14 17	17 32	..	18 10	..	21 34	..	..	..	
10	ROCKINGHAM	..	..	07 29	..	10 38	..	14 33	17 46	..	18 24	..	..	..	..	..	
14	SEATON	..	03b36	07 37	..	10 45	..	14 44	17 55	..	18 33	..	21 54	..	..		
17	WAKERLEY & BARROWDEN	d	..	07 42	..	..	..	14 49	..	..	18 38	..	..				
21¼	KING'S CLIFFE	d	..	07 50	..	10 56	..	14 57	..	18 06	18 46	..	..				
33¼	PETERBOROUGH EAST	a	04 12	08 08	..	11 12	..	15 15	18 24	..	19 04	..	22 34	..	..	..	

Saturdays | Sundays

				E		G		K		L			H ⊠			J		
BIRMINGHAM NEW STREET	d	..	..		08 50	..	09/38	..	10 50	12 30	15 58	..	..	19 38	..	00 15	..
RUGBY MIDLAND	d	02 42	06 36	..	09 51	..	10/36	..	12 33	13 47	17 00	..	17 28	..	20 52	..	02 42
LEICESTER LONDON ROAD	d	02 13	06t40	..	10t02	..			12 45		16 48	..	17 20	..	20 48	..	02 05
MARKET HARBOROUGH	d	03 15	07 15	..	10 27	..	11/25	..	13 12	14 20	17 32	..	18 10	..	21 34	..	03 15
ROCKINGHAM	d	..	07 29	..	10 38	..			13 27		17 46	..	18 24	..	..		
SEATON	d	03b36	07 37	..	10 45	..			13b37	14 42	17 55	..	18 33	..	21 54	..	03b36
WAKERLEY & BARROWDEN	d	..	07 42	..					13 42			..	18 38	..	..		
KING'S CLIFFE	d	..	07 50	..	10 56	..			13 51		18 06	..	18 46	..	..		
PETERBOROUGH EAST	a	04 12	08 08	..	11 12	..			14 11	15 09	18 24	..	19 04	..	22 34	..	04 12

Heavy figures denote through carriages
Light figures denote connecting services
For general notes see page 2

A From Yarmouth Vauxhall dep. 07 25 (Table 50)
⊠ from Norwich
B From Ely dep. 12 24 (Table 50)
C From Harwich Town dep. 12 40 (Table 50)
D 26 June to 11 September.
Through train Yarmouth Vauxhall dep. 11 40 to Walsall arr. 17 06 (Table 50)

E To March arr. 08 38 (Table 50)
G To Ely arr. 12 02 (Table 50)
H To Yarmouth Vauxhall arr. 21 53 (Table 50)
⊠ to Norwich
J Via Stamford Town (Table 52)
K Until 4 September.
Through train Walsall dep. 09 05 to Yarmouth Vauxhall arr. 14 50 (Table 42)
L Until 11 September is through train to Ipswich arr. 16 39 (Table 50)
N 10 July to 4 September.
From Yarmouth Vauxhall dep. 14 40 (Table 50)

b Arr. 3 minutes earlier
f Tuesdays and Wednesdays arr. 15 30
g Thursdays only
h Arr. Seaton 20 41
t Second class only

June 1965

PETERBOROUGH WEST

115. A saddle tank stands by the buffers at the end of the NVR in June 1994, as no. 150229 crosses the Nene, having run under the East Coast Main Line. (P.Jones)

XXV.   The track diagram is from 2006. This station saw its first train on Saturday 24th May 1986. The royal opening was by HRH Prince Edward on 30th June of that year. The suffix was changed to West from the name of the railway from April 2016, at least in the timetables. (© TRACKmaps)

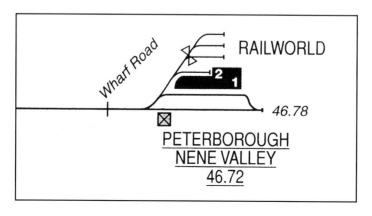

116. The saddle tank on the right of the last picture is on the left of this one, which features the popular *Flying Scotsman* on a visit in 1994. It frequently ran over the bridge on the left in its working life. (P.Jones)

117. At the other end of the station loop on the same day is no. 40106 *Atlantic Conveyor* with a demonstration freight train. The signal box is Woodston Wharf, mentioned earlier, but is out of use. It had been moved from Welland Bank, near Spalding, to the original site. (P.Jones)

118. Railworld is in the far background as we approach the terminus on 7th May 2016 in a Mk I coach. Nearer is the impressive wide range of stock stored by the NVR here, awaiting restoration. The white coach is larger in picture 120 and is elevated because it is on a levitation track, being one part of a proposed hovertrain. (V.Mitchell)

119. This picture from the same day is to show the close relationship of the NVR station with the impressive display in Railworld, shown in the next view. The water tank on the left arrived from Barking, in Essex, in July 1987. (V.Mitchell)

120. Between 1966 and 1973, Tracked Hovercraft Ltd, a government-funded company, pioneered the concept of the hovertrain at its Earith test centre, near Cambridge. Powered by a linear induction motor and supported on an air cushion, RTV 31 reached 107mph. The project, however, failed to attract anticipated commercial backing. The unit (seen above) arrived at Railworld in 1995 and stands on concrete track beams, made by Costain-Dowmac at Tallington, near Peterborough. Also on show, but not pictured, is Birmingham International Airport Maglev car no. 01 of 1984, supplied by Metro-Cammell - the world's first train without wheels in commercial service. Railworld promotes 'Sustainable Transport' with emphasis on the rail industry. It has a superb 45mm to 1ft model railway (as seen here), a tranquil nature haven and a variety of unique exhibits. (www.pboro.co.uk)

MP Middleton Press

EVOLVING THE ULTIMATE RAIL ENCYCLOPEDIA

Easebourne Midhurst GU29 9AZ. Tel:01730 813169

www.middletonpress.co.uk   email:info@middletonpress.co.uk
A-978 0 906520 B- 978 1 873793 C- 978 1 901706 D-978 1 904474
E - 978 1 906008   F - 978 1 908174